The Balance of Nature's Polarities in New-Paradigm Theory

The Reshaping of Psychoanalysis From Sigmund Freud to Ernest Becker

Barry R. Arnold
General Editor

Vol. 6

PETER LANG
New York • Washington, D.C./Baltimore • San Francisco
Bern • Frankfurt am Main • Berlin • Vienna • Paris

Dirk Dunbar

The Balance of Nature's Polarities in New-Paradigm Theory

PETER LANG
New York • Washington, D.C./Baltimore • San Francisco
Bern • Frankfurt am Main • Berlin • Vienna • Paris

Library of Congress Cataloging-in-Publication Data

Dunbar, Dirk.
The balance of nature's polarities in new-paradigm theory / Dirk Dunbar.
p. cm. — (The reshaping of psychoanalysis; Vol. 6)
Includes bibliographical references.
1. Philosophy of nature—History. 2. Ecofeminism—History.
3. Patriarchy—History. 4. Holism—History. 5. Paradigm (Theory of knowledge)—History. I. Title. II. Series.
BD581.D86 1994 113—dc20 93-31503
ISBN 0-8204-2310-6 CIP
ISSN 1059-3551

Die Deutsche Bibliothek-CIP-Einheitsaufnahme

Dunbar, Dirk:
The balance of nature's polarities in new-paradigm theory / Dirk Dunbar.
- New York; San Francisco; Bern; Baltimore; Frankfurt am Main; Berlin; Wien; Paris: Lang, 1994
(The reshaping of psychoanalysis; Vol. 6)
ISBN 0-8204-2310-6
NE: GT

Author photograph by Mark Tenney.

Cover design by James F. Brisson.

The paper in this book meets the guidelines for permanence and durability of the Committee on Production Guidelines for Book Longevity of the Council on Library Resources.

Printed in the United States of America.

To Leo, Betty, and the renewal of Earth Wisdom.

Contents

Preface

> . . . if the postmodern mind has sometimes been prone to a dogmatic relativism and a compulsively fragmenting skepticism, and if the cultural ethos that has accompanied it has sometimes deteriorated into cynical detachment and spiritless pastiche, it is evident that the most significant characteristics of the larger postmodern intellectual situation—its pluralism, complexity, and ambiguity—are precisely the characteristics necessary for the potential emergence of a fundamentally new form of intellectual vision, one that might both preserve and transcend the current state of extraordinary differentiation.[1]

The collective psyche of the twentieth century has endured an onslaught of disconnected information and an unrelenting cultivation of obsessive skepticism. Entangled by deconstruction and quantum theories, bombarded by mass media, debilitated by chaos and spiritual atrophy, the postmodern mind is plagued by fragmentation, disassociation, uncertainty, and subjectivism. According to Rollo May, the most common psychological ailment shared by people today is an engulfing sense of meaninglessness. An obvious reason for this is, as Gertrude Stein proclaims, nothing in the twentieth century agrees with anything else. Because of the indefatigable pluralism, not only has a postmodern worldview been made impossible, reality and human understanding of it have been revealed as relative and interdependent. Truth in the postmodern world is a matter of perspective.

While the conformation of the postmodern mind has involved processes both tumultuous and excruciating, it has also created immense transformative potential. This potential is made particularly explicit in terms of the reshaping of psychoanalysis. By virtue of its ability to transfigure what the West for centuries had endorsed as the self, the very founding of psychoanalysis helped create the postmodern mind. Sigmund Freud regarded the birth of psychoanalysis as the third revelation—the first being Copernicus's heliocentric cosmology and the second being Darwin's theory of evolution—which undermined the

West's millenia-long illusion of humankind's self-acclaimed ultimate place beneath God in the universe. Indeed, as Richard Tarnas explains, "Freud stood directly in the Copernican lineage of modern thought that progressively relativized the status of the human being. And again, like Copernicus and like Kant but on an altogether new level, Freud brought the fundamental recognition that the apparent reality of the objective world was being unconsciously determined by the condition of the subject." The awareness of and the attempt to recover the unconscious, which quickly became "the modern psychological imperative," stands as the "epochal insight" which has unleashed the transrational dimension of the postmodern mind.[2]

Despite Freud's insights, success, and influence, his theory of the psyche has been criticized for being too mechanistic, too grounded in patriarchal thinking. Depicting the psyche as an organ which when improperly functioning needs to be fixed, Freud followed the scientism of his day to the point of propagating a deterministic psychology. Recognizing that the conscious rational self bound so closely to the reality principle was driven by unconscious realities, he nevertheless confined his vision of the psyche by reducing it to a conglomeration of mechanical properties which are the objects of rational analysis. It was Freud's reductionist presuppositions which inevitably alienated him from his colleague Carl Jung. More than any other concept, Jung's collective unconscious liberated psychoanalysis from the realm of nineteenth-century scientism. The guardian of the archetypes, the collective unconscious has forced a reconsideration of psychic activity evolving from entities such as the id to the mystically inclined aspects of the self. While Freud recognized the reality of a "collective mind," his depiction of it was strictly concerned with sexuality—e.g., he considered the hierarchical system of reproduction of the primal horde as the source of the Oedipal Complex. A crucial example of the differences between Freud and Jung involves the Great Mother archetype. Freud explained that the "oceanic feeling" of oneness with the feminine principle was the result of, ultimately, breast feeding. Jung, on the other hand, regarded the Archetypal Feminine as a primal pattern of human awareness which transcends the ego in the embrace of universal identity. This pattern and its predispositions toward spiritual cultivation, Jung argued, has been woefully suppressed in modern Western society.

The differences between the perspectives of Freud and Jung are mirrored in many respects by the findings of the new physics and the philosophical observations in the field of epistemology. As Fritjof Capra observes, the psychoanalytic shift of emphasis from Freud's reality principle to Jung's collective unconscious finds a counterpart in the shift from classical to quantum physics. Human understanding of both the mental and physical realms has been forced to recognize and accept phenomena such as relativity, imagination, and the participatory nature and interconnectedness of reality. A similar kind of understanding links the theories of postmodern psychologists and epistemologists–namely, that the recognition of the metaphorical nature of truth has transformed the understanding of the relationship between the intellect and intuition. In Tarnas's words, "The postmodern philosopher's recognition of the inherently metaphorical nature of philosophical and scientific statements (Feyerabend, Barbour, Rorty) has been both affirmed and more precisely articulated with the postmodern psychologist's insight into the archetypal categories of the unconscious that condition and structure human experience and cognition (Jung, Hillman)."[3] The point is, a very critical phase in the reshaping of psychoanalysis, one which started with the split between the perspectives of Freud and Jung, coincided with reshapings in other fields of thought which–when effectively amalgamated–could help transform the postmodern mind.

The potential for this transformation becomes particularly clear when one acknowledges the way in which psychoanalysis' depiction of the self experienced a metamorphosis in the 1960s. The source of the human-potential movement and, hence, intricately tied to the rise of the counterculture and the New Age movement, the search for self-actualization by–among others–depth, humanistic, and transpersonal psychologists became a mainstream endeavor. Holistic therapies such as yoga, Gestalt therapy, encounter groups, and T-groups attempted to open up the postmodern mind in hopes of making new connections, of establishing a new source for inner and communal reconciliations. The greatest achievement of the human-potential movement involved its role in generating the emergence of the psychoanalytic perspectives which resulted from the cultivation of femininist and ecological sensibilities. These sensibilities have, as Tarnas explains, "brought forth the most vigorous, subtle, and radically critical analysis of conventional intellectual and cultural assumptions in all of contemporary scholarship."[4]

The visions and scholarship of feminist theorists and philosophically focused ecologists, which only now are being recognized and assimilated psychoanalytically, have started laying the foundations of the contemporary mind. Their coalesced claim is that in order to counteract the centuries of patriarchal dominance which aimed at controlling and exploiting both the environment and women, a new awareness of the self must occur. For feminists, this new self must incorporate the feminine principle, the creative matrix, the archetypally female side of being human which patriarchal language, history, religion, art, and science has so successfully repressed. Besides helping to ensure Jung's Mother Goddess archetype a most prominent place in psychoanalytic theory, feminists have done much to reconstitute the powers of intuition, imagination, cooperation, and reconciliation.

The same sort of reconstituted self is being constructed by scholars who are integrating ecology and psychoanalysis—the perfect example being the newly founded field of ecopsychology. Ecopsychologists such as Theodore Roszak have observed that the most crucial awareness that psychoanalysis could bring forth is an understanding of the interconnectedness of the self and the biosphere. Demanding that the natural environment receive the place it deserves in psychoanalytic theory, ecopsychologists proclaim that the fundamental alienation that needs immediate attention is the traditionally cultivated gulf between human nature and nature at large. In other words, with the gradual evolution of the realms of psychoanalysis from the couch to the family to the city to the universe, it has become clear that the contemporary task for psychoanalysis is to embrace feminist and ecological perspectives and continue to reshape its understanding of the self.

The processes necessary for the transformation of the postmodern mind are, then, inevitably linked to the processes which will determine the further reshaping of psychoanalysis. This book presents a vivid picture of the reshaping in two distinct ways. First, the attempt to describe what so-called new-paradigm scholars consider to be a cultural transformation–or, the creation of a wiser and kinder society more in touch with feminine virtues and ecological consciousness–takes its cue from the psychoanalytic diagnosis of the West's unconscious-repressing ego consciousness, or, a spiritually bankrupt psyche. Carl Jung, Erich Neumann, Mircea Eliade, Joseph Campbell, Alan Watts, Sam Keen, Fritjof Capra, Theodore Roszak, Riane Eisler and other scholars whom I discuss all counter the diagnosis with psychoanalytic insights designed to heal what each of them regard as an imbalanced psyche.

Second, the delineation of the three periods of the new-paradigm tradition corresponds to three discernible periods of psychology, periods which describe the field's reshaping. The seminal period begins with what Joseph Campbell calls "folk psychology" and is represented here by J. J. Bachofen. Bachofen's elucidation of the difference between Old World Eastern matriarchal and Western patriarchal "myths and mind-sets" not only influenced–as both admit–Jung and Neumann, it laid the foundation for Campbell's explication of the psychological/mythological distinctions between planters and hunters. Also part of the psychological dimension of the seminal period which I discuss is Friedrich Nietzsche's reconstruction of the Dionysian and Apollonian impulses. Nietzsche not only presents the impulses as psychological archetypes, his description of the nature of Apollo and Dionysus contains striking resemblances to Freud's super-ego and id, respectively.

The second or formational period is centered on Jungian psychology. The focus here is on the relationship between Eastern thought, archetypes (particularly the Great Mother), and the formulation of depth psychology. By synthesizing Eastern philosophies and archetypes to create alternative views of and potentially healing prescriptions for the Western psyche, the Eranos proceedings institutionalized new-paradigm thinking. In so doing, the scholars involved in the proceedings–such as Jung, Neumann, Eliade, and Campbell—anticipated the philosophy behind the 1960s spiritual revolution. While the assimilation of the East's reverence for life's balance fostered ecological consciousness, the awareness of the need to reintegrate the Mother Goddess archetype fueled the advocacy of feminine virtues.

The third or culminating period reflects the explosion of pychoanalytic perspectives and practices that promote a balanced self, or, a transformed Western psyche. The institionalization of the new theories and practices occurred with the establishment of the Esalen Institute. It was here that the search for self-actualization climaxed and generated the current reshaping of psychoanalysis. Along with the development and influence of the feminist and ecological movements, the proliferation of new psychoanalytic theories and practices has provided scholars with the means to digest, critique, sophisticate, and promote the alternative visions of the self propagated by the 1960s spiritual revolution.

Introduction

Earth Wisdom, Western Values, and the 1960s (The Three Paradigms of Cultural Transformation Theory)

> We hear a lot today about "paradigms," and especially about "new and higher" paradigms—"supertheories" that would include, beyond the physical sciences, the higher knowledge claims of philosophy-psychology and transcendental-mystical religion—a type of truly unified world view. The vision itself is fascinating: finally, an overall paradigm or theory that would unite science, philosophy-psychology, and religion-mysticism; finally, a truly "unified field theory"; finally, a comprehensive overview. Some very skilled, very sober, very gifted scholars, from all sorts of different fields, are today talking exactly that.[1]

A growing number of contemporary scholars who urge world peace and a renewed reverence for nature argue that Western culture is reintegrating a feminine, ecological impulse into its dominantly masculine, rational value system. Although the scholars describe this reintegration in diverse ways, they have located a common obstacle and solution. The obstacle is the historical valorization of the traditionally cultivated virtues associated with reason, order, control, competition, and progress. The pursuit of these virtues has created, the scholars contend, a fragmented self and an imbalanced society resulting from an unhealthy relationship to nature. From Plato's elevation of the Forms over matter to Paul's demonization of instinct to Descartes' relegation of body to spirit, Western thought has established a system of binary opposites and incessantly valued one side at the expense of the other. By suppressing phenomena such as intuition, mystery, ecstasy, communion, and spontaneity, the West has nurtured an Apollonian model of being human. The result, the scholars agree, equals a fundamental mismanagement of human potential—or, as Fritjof Capra describes it, "a crisis of perception."

The solution to the purported crisis, the scholars submit, resides in the West's continuing to cultivate a new awareness of the interrelationship between self, society, and cosmos. This new awareness is regarded among many of these scholars as the beginning of a "paradigm shift," a term instituted by Thomas Kuhn in his preface to the second edition of *The Structure of Scientific Revolutions*. For Kuhn paradigms are derived from "universally recognized scientific achievements that for a time provide model problems and solutions to a community of practitioners."[2] New-paradigm scholars have extended Kuhn's notion of a paradigm shift in science to one that addresses all relevant aspects of the purported cultural transformation. This would not only include shifts in psychology, politics, economics, medicine, art, and religion, but a master paradigm that would recognize the interdependence of these fields.

The scholars' solutions center on the principle of balance. They describe the evolution of humankind's relationship to balance in the form of three specific, chronologically arranged paradigms. The primal paradigm, known as Earth wisdom, represents the original awareness of balance—an awareness supremely expressed in the Chinese concepts yin and yang, the Indian gods Shiva and Vishnu, and the Greek gods Dionysus and Apollo. The scholars recognize Dionysus, Shiva, and/or yin as nature's feminine, dark, mysterious, and ecstatic force which exists interdependently with the masculine, light, rational, and civilizing force associated with Apollo, Vishnu, and/or yang. Expressions of a healthy balance, the cooperative opposites serve as new-paradigm models.

The second paradigm, characterized by the loss of balance, originated with Greek philosophy, matured in Roman Stoic values and Christianity, and crystalized in the Cartesian/Newtonian worldview. Cultivating the masculine over the feminine principle, this tradition fostered the manipulation of nature by erasing the primal notion of balance with antagonistic polarities. The absolute dichotomies—such as control and ecstasy, God and the Devil, and order and chaos—symbolize the West's obsession with the Ideal Good. The vehicle for the cultivation of these dichotomies has been the concept "logos." Institutionalized by Greek philosophers, Christian Church fathers, and scientific methodology, logos has evolved from Plato's rationality manifest in existence, to Paul's transcendent divine mind, to Descartes' linking of ultimate knowledge to spirit. All three meanings reflect the West's reason-as-virtue paradigm.

The third or new paradigm, which promotes the renewal of balance, was initiated by the spiritual revolution of the 1960s. Hoping to heal the split caused by the multimillenarian eulogy of reason, the sixties counterculture attempted to revitalize the Dionysian impulse in its fashion, music, literature, and lifestyle. Synthesizing and articulating relevant countercultural sensibilities, new-paradigm scholars invariably coalesce the movements and/or ideologies involving peace, human/animal rights, feminism, ecology, the Greens, Eastern religions, and transpersonal psychology. The scholars not only theorize the principle of balance, they have also used it to seed their activism.

The scholars share the conviction that the success of the cultural transformation would ensure the survival of the biosphere. Convinced that Western civilization's unrelenting embrace of masculine ideals is responsible for the subjugation of spiritual endeavor to technological progress and for phenomena such as crime, starvation, ecological and economic disasters, ill health in epidemic proportions, and the threat of nuclear war, the scholars regard as necessary the dissolution of the dominant reason-as-virtue paradigm.

Because of this conviction, new-paradigm scholars are regarded often, albeit inappropriately, as New Agers. Indisputably, the new paradigm's cultural transformation theory shares many of the views and values expounded by the New Age movement: Eastern philosophy, the Mother Goddess archetype, and holistic health practices as well as the critique of the West's overemphasis on analysis and progress. New-paradigm scholars, however, are quick to separate themselves from New Agers. Two declared reasons stem from the association of the New Age with futuristic idealism and with tricks and devices for quick spirituality.

The futuristic idealism of the New Age, based on the belief that proper use of technology will resolve the "world's ills," is—as Bill Devall and George Sessions propose in *Deep Ecology*—an extension of the patriarchal worldview:

> The New Age movement is a powerful and vocal force in today's world of futurologists and "think tanks." One reason it is so influential is that it is telling people what they are used to hearing: more and more massive technology and conquest of the planet and outer space. This is merely the most sophisticated and glamorous thrust of the Western tradition of anthropocentric domination and control.[3]

Many scholars find the New Age's unconditional faith in technology antithetical to new-paradigm perspectives. One reason, as Alan Watts explains, is that Western technology's aim "to make the world a better place" ignores the importance of the relationship between humankind and nature. The assumption that there is something *wrong* with nature—while supporting its manipulation—fosters the illusion that people are *not* "one and the same process as the universe."[4]

While the New Agers' visions of a technologically created utopia has raised serious concerns, it is their nondiscursive treatment of spirituality which has served as the focal point of new-paradigm scholars' attacks. In fact, the lack of discernment regarding spirituality has troubled most and lost many of the New Age's early advocates. In her 1987 introduction to *The Aquarian Conspiracy* (which was published in 1980 and has been regarded as the New Age handbook), Marilyn Ferguson admits that the new paradigm is being "co-opted, trivialized, exploited" by members of her own camp.[5] According to Fritjof Capra, because of the exploitation, the term New Age now refers to "people who are still New Agers, who are stuck in the consciousness of the 1970s"; while the New Age itself equals "a particular manifestation of the social paradigm shift, a manifestation that flourished in California in the 1970s and no longer exists in its original form."[6]

The tricks and devices promising spiritual enlightenment characterize the lack of rigor in the movement. The euphoric regard for its potpourri of mysticism has given the New Age a cult-mentality image. This image, which has cast a shadow over the work of new-paradigm scholars, is evident in the New Age's purported "tradition." While ideologies from, for instance,

Ralph Waldo Emerson and the Transcendentalists, William James and the "American Society for Psychical Research," Aldous Huxely, Alan Watts, Fritjof Capra and the Esalen Institute fit into both the New Age movement and the new-paradigm tradition, certain beliefs, practices, groups, and individuals such as reincarnation, channelling, parapsychology, Mesmerism, Theosophists, Rosicrucians, Urantia, Emanuel Swedenbourg, and Edgar Cayce not only lie outside the scope of new-paradigm scholarship, they support the cult-mentality image. This may sound unfair to the New Ager who has maintained a more discerning eye, but the so-called tradition is not really a tradition. Its philosophy lacks a center as well as parameters, and—at least for what has come to be known as the New Age—almost anything iconoclastic will do.

Unlike the New Age movement, new-paradigm scholarship has a clearly defined philosophy. Furthermore, this philosophy is not only shared by new-paradigm scholars, it is corroborated—as this book endeavors to show—by the various manifestations of the Dionysus/Shiva/yin impulse in the contemporary age.

Part One surveys the three periods of the new-paradigm tradition. The seminal period, which extends from the middle of the nineteenth century to the early 1930s, is composed of scholars such as Friedrich Nietzsche, Ralph Waldo Emerson, and J. J. Bachofen. While Nietzsche's Dionysus/ *Übermensch*, Emerson's Brahman/pantheism, and Bachofen's Great Mother archetype serve as model new-paradigm subjects, their discursive, poetical styles typify the approach shared by the visionary scholars of the first period. With some adjustment to Bachofen's theory (which I shall discuss later), their individual visions unite in at least two significant ways: to warn of the dangers of maintaining the reason-as-virtue paradigm and to supply sketches of a new value system.

The second or formational stage of the tradition is represented by scholars such as Carl Jung, Erich Neumann, Mircea Eliade, Alan Watts, and Joseph Campbell. These scholars were convinced that a successful reintegration of the Dionysus/Shiva/yin impulse necessitates the dissolution of beliefs which split spirit and matter, the sacred and the profane, as well as fact and value. Using Eastern philosophy and archetypes such as the Great Mother to confront and resolve the imbalance inherent in Christian mythology and scientific methodology, they condemned the following two myths: that the Judeo-Christian concept of a male God residing above his creation and rewarding and punishing his creatures provides an appropriate metaphor for the relationship of humans to the divine; and that science possesses the ability to discover ultimate truths objectively, through a value-free method. Besides anticipating major points of attack in the sixties revolution, the formational period helped to institutionalize new-paradigm thinking. The institutionalization began with the Eranos conferences initiated in 1933 and culminated in the Esalen Institute which was established in 1962.

The contemporary or culminating period which began in the sixties is epitomized by the belief that the reintegration of feminine virtues and ecological awareness is taking place. By explicating the necessity of the new-paradigm shift, the forms it is taking, and the principles behind its various manifestations, the scholars of this period have fashioned an interdisciplinary description of the sixties Zeitgeist, a spirit which inspired Esalen. The proliferation of psychological perspectives and practices involving humanistic and transpersonal psychology, mysticism, and holistic therapies (including Gestalt therapy, encounter groups, and T-groups) was ignited by the Institute. As an indication of the significance of Esalen in the articulation of the cultural transformation theory, the list of new-paradigm scholars who have served as seminar leaders there includes Aldous Huxley, Abraham Maslow, Alan Watts, Gregory Bateson, Joseph Cambell, Sam Keen, Theodore Roszak, and Fritjof Capra.

In short, the aim of Part One is to establish that there exists a rich philosophical tradition which, in the second quarter of this century, anticipated the principles behind the 1960s revolution and, now, as the century closes, is still explicating ways in which the Zeitgeist spread and continues to spread ecological awareness and feminine virtues.

While Part One shows that the awareness of and reverence for nature's balance unites the messages of all new-paradigm scholars, Part Two examines the broad spectrum of the scholars' themes, perspectives, and fields in order to give an overview of new-paradigm scholarship and to survey the scholars' uses of the primal expressions of nature's balance. For instance, Friedrich Nietzsche and Sam Keen construct their models of the transformation on a reintegration of the Dionysian impulse; Erich Neumann, Theodore Roszak, and Riane Eisler concentrate on the Mother Goddess figure (including her male satellites, Dionysus and Shiva); and Alan Watts and Fritjof Capra emphasize the yin qualities. The differences regarding the scholarly angles and perceptions are crucial because the various primal expressions not only serve as unique lenses into the dynamics of balance, but each particular view simultaneously supports new-paradigm theory and broadens its perspective.

Part Three focuses on ways in which the 1960s Zeitgeist not only embodied the Dionysus/Shiva/yin impulse, but embedded it in contemporary Western culture. The introduction to Part Three briefly describes the relationship between the sixties communal-consciousness awakening and the past forms and emerging patterns of the new paradigm. The final two chapters (Eleven and Twelve) examine ways in which the reintegration of the Dionysus/Shiva/yin impulse has occurred in the aesthetic mediums of literature and music.

More specifically, Chapter Eleven juxtaposes the philosophy and aims of the beat generation as reflected in Jack Kerouac's *Dharma Bums* with the effects of the sixties revolution as presented in Robert Pirsig's *Zen and the Art of Motorcycle Maintenance*. The purpose here is to show how the rebellion dramatized by Kerouac was based on Dionysian/erotic *forms* (orgies, anti-intellectualism, anti-establishment behavior), whereas Pirsig's message represented a return to Dionysian/erotic *principles* such as self-understanding and finding the *daimon* within.

Chapter Twelve describes the evolution of the rock-and-roll cult into a movement and the way the messages in the songs gradually became more sophisticated in scope and aim. I shall begin by comparing rock-and-roll and Dionysianism in terms of structural relationships (particularly the intoxicating effect of their musical instruments, the ecstatic nature of their dances, and the evolution of their uses of language), and conclude with interpretations of relevant rock-and-roll lyrics which propagate values reflective of the new paradigm.

In sum, by examining and synthesizing the theories of new-paradigm scholars, I intend not only to focus the message of new-paradigm scholarship, but to describe how the rise of reason in the West forced the Dionysus/Shiva/yin impulse underground for over two millenia, until the spiritual revolution of the 1960s initiated an extensive attempt to reintegrate it. In other words, beginning with the delineation of the three periods of the tradition, turning to the individual theories, and ending with manifestations of the new paradigm which corroborate the theories, this book explains how the crises indicative of the contemporary age have solutions which were prophesied in the modern age and are being recognized now.

I

THE THREE PERIODS OF THE NEW-PARADIGM MESSAGE

> We believe . . . that we may not need something new, but need to reawaken something very old, to reawaken our understanding of Earth wisdom. In the broadest sense, we need to accept the invitation to the dance—the dance of unity of humans, plants, animals, the Earth. We need to cultivate an ecological consciousness. And we believe that a way out of our present predicament may be simpler than many people realize.[1]

New-paradigm scholars tend to use phrases like, "I believe," "it is my conviction," and "I am convinced." Part of the reason is that concepts such as "Zeitgeist," "Earth wisdom," and "the values of Western civilization"—the amorphous subjects of their inquiries—are intangible, unverifiable phenomena. The awareness of a Zeitgeist, for instance, requires an intuitive leap from social/political events, discoveries, inventions, and works of art to ideologies, movements, and other collective ways of seeing. When the logical pitfalls of comparing two or more Zeitgeists are added, a process which makes connections even more tenuous and increases the necessity and illusiveness of definitions, what remain are helplessly subjective conclusions. "Yet," as Theodore Roszak explains, "that elusive conception called 'the spirit of the times' continues to nag at the mind and demand recognition, since it seems to be the only way available in which one can make even provisional sense of the world one lives in."[2] Or, as Carl Jung more pronouncedly concludes in *The Undiscovered Self*: "The unconscious Zeitgeist . . . compensates the attitude of the conscious mind and anticipates changes to come."[3]

New-paradigm scholars very often counteract the speculative nature of their conclusions in prefaces, forewords, and/or introductions with their own formulation of one or more of the following claims: details and facts are important, but they render the phenomena in dissected parts, whereas "I" propose to capture its spirit (e.g., Nietzsche and Watts); "my" topic is broad and "my" findings are based on personal experience, but the significance and applicability of both to the present social crises hopefully outweighs the inevitable generalizations (Jung and Keen); "my" aim is not to present a solution, but to clear some of the ground for future scholars (Neumann and Roszak); "my" project, not the vision, is incomplete (Eliade and Capra). Such claims are also used to justify the new-paradigm scholar's approach and style.[4]

Obviously, not all new-paradigm scholars share the same approach and style; however, they inevitably take the same kind of liberties and break the same kind of conventions in expressing their message. The term which the creators of new-paradigm language have instituted to express the unconventional nature of their study is "holistic." Derived from the Greek term *holos*, holism refers to an understanding of reality which cannot be divided into constituent parts. The scholars maintain that the recognition of holistic properties demands the use of intuition, a mode of cognition which complements the rational intellect. While the rational means of knowing is associated with the linear, analytic ability to "breakdown," classify, and logically apprehend, intuitive understanding results from a direct, insight-oriented experience. Intuitive truth can neither be acheived through analysis, nor explained through the conventional use of words.

Ralph Waldo Emerson was one of the first scholars to use a holistic style and approach to formulate his new-paradigm message. Convinced that truth demanded it, Emerson sacrificed scholarly argument for persuasive prose. While the poet "can integrate all the parts," the conventional use of words "cannot cover the dimensions of what is in truth. They break, chop, and impoverish it."[5] He not only wrote poetry, he managed to minimize the possibility of breaking and chopping the ideas he expressed in his prose by denying the reader (as best he could) a position from which to discern his meaning through proof, consistency, or logic. Very simply, Emerson intended his message to be intuited and felt rather than analyzed and rationally comprehended.

Friedrich Nietzsche, who called Emerson "the most insightful author of this century thus far," used the same kind of approach and style.[6] As I will show in Chapter Four, Nietzsche's writing, much like Emerson's, evokes a skeptical attitude regarding the capability of language to capture his meaning in all but one way, holistically.

The scholars of the second or formational stage of the new-paradigm tradition also implemented a holistic approach to develop their messages. However, the scholars of this period benefited from the establishment of a new language, the language of symbols, archetypes, and the collective unconscious. As holistic a concept as the Zeitgeist, the collective unconscious represents humankind's psychic connection to its earliest, most primitive images of reality. As the contents or primordial images of the collective unconscious, archetypes equal innate human patterns and forms for perceiving the world and serve as predispositions for interacting with it. The symbols which represent or (in Jung's words) "belong to" archetypes are particularly relevant to psychological interpretations of mythology. For instance, the vessel–which, as Erich Neumann explains, serves as a manifestation "of the Archetypal Feminine in all times and all cultures"–appears "in the living reality of the modern woman, in her dreams and visions, compulsions and fantasies, projections and relationships, fixations and transformations."[7] In other words, the holistic language of the second period addresses in an altogether new way the awareness of the West's need to reintegrate feminine virtues.

Despite the creation of the new language, the psychological inquiry has as its object a transpersonal dimension which can be approached holistically, but in a necessarily cautious manner–as Neumann affirms:

> The problem of the creative unconscious, the central problem of depth psychology, is at the same time the central problem of mysticism and mystical man. Since the creative process takes place outside of consciousness and must therefore be looked upon as an experience at

> the limits of the ego, any attempt to approach this central and primal vortex is a hazardous undertaking. It is in the very nature of such an undertaking that its object cannot be captured by the direct intervention of consciousness, but that one must seek to approach the center in question by a sort of ritual circling, an approach from many sides.[8]

Problems and inadequacies included, concepts such as the Archetypal Masculine and Archetypal Feminine supplied new-paradigm theory with a whole new framework with which to discuss realities of an intrinsically holistic nature.

The holistic essence of the contemporary new-paradigm inquiries is exhibited by the variety of the scholars' approaches. More numerous, more interdisciplinary, and more emphatic about their message, contemporary new-paradigm scholars weave their perspectives around a multitude of holistically apprehended realities. Humanistic and transpersonal psychologists, cultural historians and ethnologists, quantum physicists, molecular biologists, feminist archaeologists, eco-ethicists, and comparative religionists are some of the scholars who are creating an intellectual rapprochement based on a thematic unity. Compared to the scholars of the other two periods, contemporary new-paradigm scholars cover a wider range of topics and, yet, tend to be the most focused on establishing the inevitable message: individuals and societies in the West could enhance the quality of life by reintegrating the Dionysus/Shiva/yin impulse.

1

Seminal Visions of a Balanced Self: The Theories of Emerson, Nietzsche, and Bachofen

> The Transcendentalist adopts the whole connection of spiritual doctrine. . . . he believes in inspiration, and in ecstasy . . . . You will see by this sketch that there is no such thing as a Transcendental party; that there is no pure Transcendentalist; that we know of none but prophets and heralds of such a philosophy.[1]

The aim of seminal new-paradigm scholars was to create a model of a balanced self, a self which mirrors the union of nature's polarities. Two visionaries united in this aim were Ralph Waldo Emerson and Friedrich Nietzsche. While Emerson's notion of balance carried Eastern overtones (e.g., the "Oversoul"), Nietzsche constructed–at least originally–his model (the "Overman") on the balance of the Greek gods Dionysus and Apollo. The model self in both of their philosophies shared the "back to nature" impulse characteristic of the Romantic and Transcendental movements. A self-acclaimed prophet of Transcendentalism, Emerson celebrated the transrational component of the human psyche and the experience of God as nature. He warned that the West's split of spirit and body encouraged a mechanized view of life and fostered the dehumanization of individuals and society.

His friend and fellow Transcendentalist Henry David Thoreau helped ignite his enthusiasm for Eastern philosophy. Although Emerson started reading the Vedas at age nineteen, his passion for, in particular, Hinduism did not begin to materialize in his work until he neared forty. Thoreau not only gave him a number of Eastern works of philosophy, he displayed his own transport in reading and discussing Eastern works with Emerson. Together they began writing about their insights in *The Dial.* Although Thoreau's use of Eastern thought (e.g., the Vedas, the *Bhagavad Gita,* Confucius, Mencius, and Chuang Tzu) centered on bolstering his own ideas, Emerson actually fused Indian concepts (e.g., Brahman and maya) into his message.

Nietzsche's philosophy, unlike Emerson's, was not part of a movement, but did relate to the same Zeitgeist. An existential neo-Romantic, Nietzsche and his vision of Dionysus brought the Romantic ideal to its darkest level, face to face with nature in its most brutal, instinctive element. His influence on and assimilation of various perspectives representative of nineteenth-century and early twentieth-century German philosophy and literature have been well noted. A particular chain of influence and assimilation, one that fascinated Carl Jung, involved Johann Wolfgang von Goethe's influence on Nietzsche and Nietzsche's influence on Herman Hesse. Versions of the same model, Goethe's Faust, Nietzsche's Zarathustra, and Hesse's Demian represent the same archetype. Lonely, amoral, mysterious, and rebellious, all three figures metaphorically embody the dark side of humankind–the side archetypally belonging to Dionysus, Abraxas, Wotan, Mephistopheles, and the Devil.

Nietzsche's connection to ideas which he modified as well as ideas that he anticipated is also manifest in the similarities between his theories and those of G. W. F. Hegel and Sigmund Freud. One of Hegel's most significant concepts, the Dialectical World Process, strongly influenced Nietzsche. Although he refuted Hegel's teleological stance (that the dialectic is part of a divine order), Nietzsche transmuted Hegel's notion of a *Weltgeist* or world spirit that dialectically evolves through the thesis, antithesis, and synthesis stages into a process that fit into his depiction of the evolution of Dionysian and Apollonian impulses through four periods of ancient Greek history (periods described in Chapter Four). The interactions in Hegel's Weltprozess reflect for Nietzsche the kinds of processes governing Dionysus and Apollo: a constant unfolding of friction and balance wherein unending change and more and more "powerful births" rule—in short, a universal rhythm. For Nietzsche, however, the West's eulogy of reason, which he chastised Hegel for promoting, disrupted the rhythm. Nietzsche criticized Hegel for the same reasons he condemned Christianity, namely, that the belief in a *Weltprozess* which has an end point to which—via the power of logos—all of life's energy is being directed is a life-denying fiction.[2]

Nietzsche's understanding of the two impulses shared many of the theoretical distinctions which Freud made between the super-ego and id. As processes reflective of the human psyche, the Apollonian super-ego serves as the conscience or source of moral standards represented by internalized voices of authority and the Dionysian id works as the basic innate element of the psyche which seeks immediate gratification of desire and attempts to eliminate or reduce tension. While the former is driven by the morality principle (or, for Nietzsche, "the Apollonian urge to correct") and the latter by the pleasure principle (or the Dionysian drive for ecstasy), it remains the duty of the ego, in Freudian terms, or the self, in Nietzschean terms, to balance the two. While the ego, grounded in the reality principle, works to temper the id and adhere to the voice of the super-ego, the balanced self in Nietzsche's philosophy integrates the rational with the ecstatic, the ordered with the chaotic, and "dreams" with "intoxication."

Although the similarities between Nietzsche's ideas and those of Freud and Hegel are more tenuous than those between Emerson and Thoreau, they signify the birth of a language for fields of study—namely, the Zeitgeist and the psyche—that, along with the ecological vision and Eastern philosophy of Transcendentalism, have characterized new-paradigm scholarship. What makes Emerson and Nietzsche particularly representative of the tradition is their use of the notion of balance. Five steps, which outline their respective messages in terms of balance, aid in establishing their similarities and, more generally, in characterizing new-paradigm scholarship. I shall discuss Nietzsche later. Here, briefly, are Emerson's steps.

First, he acknowledges nature's polarities and their interrelatedness:

> An inevitable dualism bisects nature, so that each thing is a half, and suggests another thing to make it whole; as, spirit, matter; man, woman; odd, even; subjective, objective; in, out; upper, under; motion, rest; yea, nay.
>
> Whilst the world is thus dual, so is everyone of its parts. The entire system of things gets represented in every particle.[3]

Second, he recognizes the necessity of balancing these polarities:

> Under all this running sea of circumstance, whose waters ebb and flow with perfect balance, lies the aboriginal abyss of real Being. Essence, or God, is not a relation or a part, but the whole . . . self-balanced, and swallowing up all relations, parts and times within itself. Nature, truth, virtue, are the influx from thence. Vice is the absence or departure of the same.[4]

Third, by subjugating intuition and instinct to intellectual powers, Western man has created a precarious imbalance:

> ". . . if still he [Western man] have elemental power . . . it is not conscious power, it is not inferior but superior to his will. It is Instinct." Thus my Orphic poet sang.
>
> At present, man applies to nature but half his force. He works on the world with his understanding alone. He lives in it and masters it by a penny-wisdom; and he that works most in it is but a half-man. . . . His relation to nature, his power over it, is through the understanding. . . . The reason why the world lacks unity, and lies broken and in heaps, is, because man is disunited with himself.[5]

Fourth, the dominance of Christianity and science sustains this imbalance. Emerson roots the failure of Christianity in what he regards as a perversion of the truth expounded by Jesus—who "saw that God incarnates himself in man, and evermore goes forth anew to take possession of his World. He said, in this jubilee of sublime emotion, 'I am divine. Through me, God acts; through me, speaks. Would you see God, see me; or see thee, when thou also thinkest as I now think.' But what a distortion did his doctrine and memory suffer in the same, in the next, and the following ages!" By portraying Jesus as a "demigod," an "Apollo," the Christian tradition "has fallen into the error that corrupts all attempts to communicate religion." While suppressing the mystical Kingdom within, it glorifies "the personal, the positive, the ritual. It has dwelt, it dwells, with noxious exaggeration about the *person* of Jesus. The soul knows no persons."[6] Science, on the other hand, lacks "sufficient humanity": "empirical science is apt to cloud the sight, and, by the very knowledge of functions and processes, to bereave the student of the manly contemplation of the whole."[7]

Fifth, Emerson draws from "Oriental" philosophy (particularly that of the "Hindoos"), Dionysianism (under the name of Bacchus, but including Pan and Orpheus), and the Great Mother impulse to support his new-paradigm model.[8] A devotee of the pantheism of all mystical traditions without elaborating on any of them, he preaches the philosophy of the East which, he implies, engendered all "Mother Earth" cults. For instance, the "Over-Soul," the title of one of his essays, is his name for Brahman–the Hindu concept that he considers among the most significant "in the history of intellect." Even more relevant is his model of the "balanced soul," which represents the integrated embodiment of Asian and European ways of understanding and interacting with the universe. In "Plato; or, the Philosopher," he refers to Asia with terms such as female, earth, unity, abstractions, ecstasy, being, soul, nature, and infinity; and to Europe with male, heaven, sun, divide, detail, discipline, and boundaries. The "defining, result-loving, machine-making, surface-seeking" West, which honors forms, transcendental distinctions, inventions, statistics, and inventories, needs a new model, a model which is prevalent in the self-reliant, ideal person whose life resounds with universal balance.[9]

Although Emerson envisioned a new paradigm, he did not conclusively formulate one: his writings are too ambiguous, his message too vague, and his references too undeveloped. His work is so open to interpretation that the Oversoul, a term he only used twice, has become an Emersonian catchword.[10] Regardless, the resurgence of interest in his work since the 1960s attests to the power of his vision. His ideas have been connected with the youth movement of the sixties, women's rights, and ecology.[11] "Emerson is being studied afresh," Hyatt Waggoner suggests, because he has "something to say that is relevant to our condition."[12]

While Emerson's and Nietzsche's philosophy anticipated new-paradigm theory, another nineteenth-century writer J. J. Bachofen dramatically influenced the role that mythology played in the formation of the tradition. In *The Mother Right: An Inquiry into the Gynocracy of the Old World in Her Religious and Legitimate Nature,* Bachofen elucidates the differences between "Old World" Eastern matriarchal (including pre-Athens Greece) and later Western patriarchal myths and culture. The distinctions he draws between the East's earth goddesses and the West's sky and sun gods have become a focal point of new-paradigm scholarship. For instance, in his book *Joseph Campbell: An Introduction*, Robert Segal maintains that both Bachofen and Campbell claim that "the prime matriarchal values are changelessness, passivity, peace, selflessness, and equality. The prime patriarchal ones are change, activity, ambition, fighting, self-centeredness, and hierarchy."[13] Although Bachofen expresses a sense of remorse at the loss of feminine values, he insists (unlike Campbell and other new-paradigm scholars) that the shift from matriarchal to patriarchal society elevated the human race to its highest and most spiritual realm.

Both Carl Jung and his colleague Erich Neumann regard Bachofen as a pioneer in the study of mythological archetypes. While Jung states that Bachofen "influenced my understanding of the nature of symbols," Neumann adds that Bachofen's "interpretation of the symbols [particularly solar and lunar] has been largely confirmed by modern depth psychology."[14] While praising Bachofen for his "myth-piercing eye," Neumann implicates him (for eulogizing the sun-masculine symbol and devaluing the moon-feminine one) in the creation of the modern consciousness which "has led to a hypertrophy of consciousness at the expense of the whole man." However, Neumann claims, if Bachofen's distinctions are "understood psychologically rather than sociologically, his discoveries have lasting value." In other words, while Bachofen's thought is often "strangely limited by patriarchal-Christian conceptions," he still manages to formulate the first archetypal understanding of the Great Mother, an archetype of profound significance for the new-paradigm's formational period.[15]

2

Eranos, the East, and the Mother Goddess Archetype: The Fusion of Psychology and Mythology in the Formulation of New-Paradigm Theory

> It is perhaps the greatest contribution of Eranos to have stimulated and encouraged meetings and dialogues among representatives of the various sciences and disciplines whose field is the human mind and spirit. For it is through such encounters that a culture can renew itself, in a bold widening of its horizon. Depth psychologists, orientalists, and ethnologists interested in the history of religions are those who have most successfully achieved rapprochement and even collaboration. This is perhaps due to the fact that, in the last analysis, each of these disciplines implies encountering and confronting an unknown, strange, even "dangerous" world–dangerous because able to threaten the spiritual equilibrium of the modern West . . . .[1]

The inquiries and aims of the second or formational period of new-paradigm scholarship were institutionalized by the proceedings of Eranos–the name (suggested by Rudolph Otto, meaning a "shared feast") given to the annual meetings begun in 1933 at Ascona, Switzerland. The brainstorm of Olga Froebe-Kapteyn, Eranos, in her words, is "greatly indebted to C. G. Jung, whose rediscovery of the archetypal world and its value for us today has from the beginning provided us with a background for the work done here in the last twenty-three years. Eranos is a cultural event; it should not be considered as a separate manifestation but as an integral part of the stream of events that expresses the culture of our times."[2] A brief examination of the topics addressed at the first six meetings sheds light on the stream of events of this period–events which

Mircea Eliade describes (in the quotation above) as endangering the West's traditional worldview.

The topic of the first meeting was "Yoga and Meditation in the East and the West." Speakers and paper titles included: Heinrich Zimmer's "On the Significance of the Indian Tantric Yoga," Erwin Rouselle's "Spiritual Guidance in Contemporary Taoism," and G. R. Heyer's "The Meaning of Eastern Wisdom for Western Spiritual Guidance."[3] The aim of the first meeting, in other words, involved the description of Eastern thought and practices as a remedy for the imbalanced Western psyche. As Joseph Campbell indicates, this aim is clearly delineated by Jung in his "opening words to the first meeting of the long and fruitful enterprise":

> The European comes seeking the perfumed air of the Orient: disagreeable, a pirate, conquistador, dripping with his "Religion of Love," an opium dealer, disoriented, poverty-stricken in spite of his wealth of knowledge and intellectual pretension. That is the picture of your Western Man. That is the reason I have set a certain motto as the foundation of my talk. You must not expect a neatly rounded lecture. Only the Orient has achieved completion: the West is a concatenation of inadequacies. My motto is to be found in Chapter 20 of the *Tao Te Ching*. There Lao-tse wrote . . . "I cherish the Bestowing Mother."[4]

The attempt to "mediate East and West" remained the aim of the next two meetings entitled "Spirtual Guidance in the East and the West" and also in the following two meetings, both entitled "The Shaping of the Idea of Redemption in the East and the West."

In 1938, however, a different, though not separate, topic was introduced, "The Configuration and Cult of the 'Great Mother.'" Speakers and paper titles included Jean Przyluski's "Origins and Development of the Cult of the Mother Goddess," Charles Picard's "The Great Mother from Crete to Eleusis," Heinrich Zimmer's "The Indian World Mother," and G. R. Heyer's "The Great Mother in the Psyche of Modern Man."[5] While the precise use of Eastern philosophy and the Great Mother archetype by new-paradigm scholars are subjects of later chapters, here the point is that the scholars who met at the Eranos conferences assimilated the philosophy and the archetype to create the conceptual tools that were implemented to confront and resolve the imbalance characteristic of the mythology, value system, and collective psyche of Western civilization.

Building their theories on psychological interpretations of mythology, the thinkers in the formational period received their inspiration from the East. Having discovered cultures that dissolved polarities, they explored the notion of antagonistic polarities in non-Greek European cultures and recognized the need to reinstate the feminine principle as a valuable asset to human potential and spiritual well-being. Finally, after discovering the psychological role of the Earth Mother, they applied it to Western culture.

This process of discovery and application of balance is nowhere clearer than in the work of Carl Jung, the *key* figure in the formation of new-paradigm scholarship. Jung expanded upon Bachofen's symbolic distinctions, delineating them as the female, Eastern, intuitive, instinctive collective unconscious and the male, Western, rational, controlled ego-consciousness. Jung insisted that these diverse components of self or psyche are depicted as archetypal images of balance in the Eastern concepts of Tao and Brahman:

> When the unconscious brings together the male and the female, things become utterly indistinguishable and we cannot say any more whether they are male or female. . . . You find the same idea in ancient Chinese philosophy. The ideal condition is named Tao, and it consists of the complete harmony between heaven and earth. . . . The idea of the union of the two opposite principles, of male and female, is an archetypal image.[6]

Furthermore:

> The primordial image underlying *rta-brahman-atman* and *tao* is as universal as man, appearing in every age and among all peoples as a primitive conception of energy, or 'soul force,' or however else it may be called. . . . Knowledge of *tao* therefore has the same redeeming and uplifting effect as the knowledge of *brahman*. . . . The aim of Taoist ethics, then, is to find deliverance from the cosmic tension of opposites by a return to *tao*.[7]

Convinced that the East offers the West a model by which to reintegrate the unconscious, Jung nevertheless warns that, because Eastern traditions would be "impossible to imitate," they should not be used to supplant Western traditions.

Rather, they "should remind us of that which is similar in our own culture and which we have already forgotten, and should direct our attention to that which we have pushed aside as insignificant, namely, the fate of our own inner man."[8]

Jung's significance in the development of new-paradigm scholarship is particularly marked by his role in the establishment of Eranos. Three of the most significant contributors to the Eranos' proceedings, Mircea Eliade, Erich Neumann, and Joseph Campbell, all regard Jung's work as the group's scholarly focal point. Campbell, the editor of a six-volume compendium of Eranos meetings, reports that the continuity of the meetings was due to "the continuous presence and genial spirit of Dr. C. G. Jung, whose concept of the fundamental psychological laws of human life and thought supplied a criterion for both the recognition and the fostering of the perennial in a period of transformation."[9]

Jung contributed to the conventions from 1933 to 1951. In 1933, the same year he published *Modern Man in Search of a Soul*, Jung shared his vision of the "whole man" in "A Study in the Process of Individuation." The individuation process, Jung claims, leads toward "wholeness," "an integration of opposites," and can be paraphrased as "Self-realization." More precisely, "If the individuation process is made conscious, consciousness must confront the unconscious and a balance between the opposites must be found. As this is not possible through logic, one is dependent on *symbols* which make the irrational union of opposites possible."[10] At the 1934 meeting, Jung delivered "The Archetypes of the Collective Unconscious" and in 1938 he presented "Psychological Aspects of the Mother Archetype." In short, Eranos, under the guidance of scholars such as Jung, helped develop new-paradigm theory in an effort to reintegrate the Dionysus/Shiva/yin impulse in Western culture.

Neumann, Eliade, and Campbell capture the spirit and embrace the framework of this development. Alone, the title of Neumann's 1953 lecture, "The Significance of the Earth Archetype for Modern Times," reflects his scholarly aim (which I shall examine later). In a 1959 introduction to the *Eranos Papers*, Eliade applauds the role both Jung and Eranos have played in helping form not only a new discipline, but a Zeitgeist which will assure the creation of a dialogue between Western society and "primitive" and Asian myths and rites.[11]

In *Patterns in Comparative Religion,* Eliade structures his discussion around hierophanies in order to examine religion's truly "unique and irreducible" element, the function of the sacred. A hierophany is "anything which manifests the sacred." He draws from hierophanies associated with male sky and female earth worship, biological rhythms (e.g., of the sun and moon), sacred places, myths and symbols to show the forms and the "dialectic of the sacred." Much like Jung, he insists "that myth reveals more profoundly than any rational experience ever could, the actual structure of the divinity, which transcends all attributes and reconciles all contraries." Amidst a myriad of examples, he uses Brahman, the Mother Goddess, Shiva and Vishnu, yin and yang, and Dionysus and Apollo to delineate mythical forms which symbolize this reconciliation. In other words, a *coincidentia oppositorum* ("a union of opposites") serves as a "mythical pattern" or an "archetypal model" of the divine.[12] As does Jung, Eliade suggests that the most eloquent versions of this model derive from the East:

> The oriental mind cannot conceive perfection unless all opposites are present in their fulness. The neophyte begins by identifying all his experience with the rhythms governing the universe (sun and moon), but once this "cosmisation" has been achieved, he turns all his efforts towards *unifying* the sun and moon, towards taking into himself the primeval unity which was before the world was made; a unity which signifies not the chaos that existed before any forms were created but the undifferentiated *being* in which all forms are merged.[13]

After describing the ontology of moon, water, and woman symbols as representing the cosmological pattern of change, regeneration, and repetition, he concludes that, "thanks chiefly to his symbols, the *real existence* of primitive man was not the broken and alienated existence lived by civilized man today."[14] The primitive and "Oriental" myths and symbols evoking the cyclical nature of time, a theme he develops in *The Myth of the Eternal Return,* display a mutual understanding of the hierophanous "center"–the undifferentiated being manifest in sacred places, the eternal present, and the archetypal nature of all religious acts. This center provided the primitive and

"Oriental" self with the magic space wherein the divine unifies opposites and renews human history. Hence, in a process of eternal renewal, the universe is reborn again and again, unlike in Christian myth. The center of Christianity rests with the rebirth of one individual, Christ, whose followers have transformed the mystery of renewal into faith in a one-time event of linear history. "In this respect," Eliade claims, "Christianity incontestibly proves to be the religion of 'fallen man': and this to the extent to which modern man is irremediably identified with history and progress, and to which history and progress are a fall, both implying the final abandonment of the paradise of archetypes and repetition."[15]

However, by virtue of the emerging interdisciplinary spirit which Eliade praises in Eranos and Jung's work, he foresees a widespread reawakening of the *coincidentia oppositorum* in Christian myth and, more generally, a rekindling of intuitive and ecstatic powers in the West. As he claims in *The Two and the One* (entitled "Mephistopheles et l'Androgyne" in the 1962 edition):

> It is not impossible that our epoch will be known to posterity as the first to rediscover the 'manifold religious experiences' which were abolished by the triumph of Christianity. . . . It appears that all these elements are preparing for the rise of a new humanism, which will not be a replica of the old, since above all it is the researches of orientalists, ethnologists, psychologists, and religious historians, which must now be integrated in order to reach a total knowledge of man.[16]

Joseph Campbell shares many of Jung's and Eliade's sentiments and professes related theories. He agrees that Eranos represents "our common task of understanding the present period of cultural catastrophe . . . and of prelude."[17] He argues that the West's catastrophic condition is the result of a spiritual ignorance concerning the function of mythology and that the emergence of a new paradigm depends upon whether or not the West can re-create an awareness of the power of myth and myths to "live by." In *The Hero with a Thousand Faces*, while presenting a myth to live by, Campbell shows how the morphology of the journey and the message of the hero archetype are the same regardless of cultural setting and costume; and that the stages of the journey–including the departure, initiation, and return—represent psychic transformations. As do Jung, Neumann, and Eliade, Campbell suggests that Christians tend to interpret literally the myths of Christ and distort thereby the archetypal meaning. Jesus' death and rebirth actually represent the crucifixion and resurrection of the ego; and, as with all heroes, the resurrected psyche/Christ bestows the divine secret of the mysterious unconscious to humankind. Jesus is not reborn historically, "but as eternal man—perfected, unspecific, universal man."[18] If properly interpreted, Christ's incarnation functions "as a mythological image transcending the popular notion of an absolute dichotomy of nature and spirit," for "in the person of Jesus not only was the idea of the absolute distinction of the opposed terms God and man refuted, but the point was also made that one should realize, like Jesus, this coincidence of opposites as the ultimate truth and substance of oneself."[19] The hero's message, then, is that the divine Kingdom is within and the coincidence of opposites governs the universe.

As Campbell explains in his four-volume work *The Masks of God*, this message dominates Eastern mythology. Claiming that the East's matriarchal, communal-oriented planting societies lived by growing food while the West's patriarchal, hierarchical-oriented hunting societies lived by killing for food, he argues that the planters nurtured a mystical unity with the gods, while the hunters retained an ontological distinction between Creator and creature. Convinced that the matriarchal societies were subsumed by hunters with their warrior sky gods, he declares that Western myths have "masked" their true Eastern essence, not only making the goddess figures subordinate, but turning them into evil enemies. As he claims in *The Masks of God: Occidental Mythology*:

> In the older mother myths and rites the light and darker aspects of the mixed thing that is life had been honored equally and together, whereas in the later, male-oriented, patriarchal myths, all that is good and noble was attributed to the new, heroic master gods, leaving to the native nature powers the character only of darkness—to which, also, a negative moral judgment now was added.[20]

In terms very similar to Eliade's, Campbell proclaims the arrival of a new scholarly spirit which aims at explaining and propagating the West's rediscovery of the mythic principles of cosmic renewal, *coincidentia oppositorum*, and the divine within. This new spirit, he suggests, is epitomized in the proceedings of Eranos: "There, year after year, successive companies of the greatest scholars of our time have assembled to compare and expound their views concerning those 'elementary forms,' informing themes and visions, creative urges and symbolic aims—the 'archetypes,' in short—that have inspired, and are inspiring still, the cultural evolution of mankind."[21] The result is that "a host of scholars" have extended the "researches begun last century in the field of folk psychology" in an attempt "to establish the psychological bases of language, myth, religion, art development, and moral codes."[22]

In an interview with Eliade conducted at an Eranos conference, Jung expounded a virtual manifesto of the formational period of new-paradigm scholarship:

> Speaking always as a psychologist, I affirm that the presence of God is manifest, in the profound experience of the psyche, as a *coincidentia oppositorum*, and the whole history of religion, all the theologies, bear witness to the fact that the *coincidentia oppositorum* is one of the commonest and most archaic formulas for expressing the reality of God. . . . The modern world is desacralized, that is why it is in a crisis. Modern man must rediscover a deeper source of his own spiritual life. To do this, he is obliged to struggle with evil, to confront his shadow, to integrate the devil. There is no other choice. That is why Yahweh, Job, Satan, represent psychologically exemplary situations: they are like paradigms of the eternal human drama.[23]

The scholars of the formational period of new-paradigm scholarship philosophically anticipated the need for the 1960s revolution. The West's overemphasis on the Apollo/Vishnu/yang principle has created an imbalance, and the clearest way—according to Jung, Neumann, Eliade, and Campbell—to resolve the imbalance is to reintegrate the Dionysus/Shiva/yin impulse by using Eastern wisdom and the Great Mother archetype as guides. Ironically, theirs was precisely the philosophy that was lacking in the beat and hippie experimentation with Eastern thought. It was not until the ecological and feminist movements joined the battle against the West's patriarchal worldview that the principles behind the sixties revolution began to be articulated in the spirit which emanated from Eranos. As a prophesy and a challenge, Eliade describes what must occur in the next period of new-paradigm theory:

> The problem that now arises—and that will present itself with even more dramatic urgency to scholars of the coming generation—is this . . . (1) Western man cannot continue to live on for an indefinite period in separation from an important part of himself, the part constituted by the fragments of a spiritual history of which he cannot decipher the meaning and message. (2) Sooner or later, our dialogue with the "others"—the representatives of traditional, Asiatic, and "primitive" cultures—must begin to take place not in today's empirical and utilitarian language (which can approach only realities classifiable as social, economic, political, sanitary, etc.) but in a cultural language capable of expressing human realities and spiritual values.[24]

The new language, which started with scholars such as Nietzsche and Emerson and was instituted by Eranos, is still being articulated in the third or culminating period.

3

Esalen and the 1960s Revolution: The Articulation of the New Values in the Contemporary Age

> Our 1960s and 1970s have generated a whole series of philosophical, spiritual, and political movements that seem to go in the same direction. They all counteract the overemphasis on yang attitudes and values, and try to reestablish a balance between the masculine and feminine sides of human nature.[1]

As Eranos helped form new-paradigm scholarship, Esalen (the name of an Amerindian tribe) heralded its culminating phase. Established by Michael Murphy and Richard Price in Big Sur, California in 1962, Esalen initiated the articulation and encouraged the practices of the philosophy behind the 1960s revolution—or, as W. T. Anderson testifies in *The Upstart Spring: Esalen and the American Awakening*: "it was a place where some of whatever it was that was happening, was happening."[2] Aldous Huxley is credited with helping to formulate the Institute's conceptual aim. This aim, the exploration and actualization of latent psychic powers (or, in Huxley's words, the study of "the nonverbal Humanities"), is reflected in some of the original topics taught there: mythology, mysticism, meditation, comparative religion, and various forms of psychotherapy and consciousness expansion. Anderson insinuates that Huxley, Murphy, and Price expected the spiritual revolution of the 1960s and anticipated Esalen's role in it.[3]

The prototype of transpersonal growth centers which have flourished since the mid-sixties, Esalen represented the cutting edge of the counterculture. Encounter groups, Gestalt workshops, yoga and t'ai-chi sessions, Rock concerts, radical political ideology, drug seminars, and a free-love attitude constituted much of Esalen's image in the sixties. A number of instructors—such as Aldous Huxley, Alan Watts, Gerald Heard, Ram Dass (Richard Alpert), Gregory Bateson, Timothy Leary, and Stanislav Grof—wrote about their studies of and exploits with consciousness-changing drugs. Alan Watts, whom Capra calls "one of the heroes of the counterculture," mixed his drug research with his understanding of Zen and Taoism, claiming that LSD offers an experience which obliterates the monotheistic West's "greatest of all superstitions," the separation of mind and the body, spirit and matter, thing and event. In the preface to Watts's *The Joyous Cosmology: Adventures in the Chemistry of Consciousness,* Dass and Leary call Watts "one of the great reporters of our times" and commend him for making "more explicit and familiar in our Western world" the apparently innate relationship between psychedelic visions and "the non-dualistic conceptions of Eastern philosophy."[4]

Despite the fact that much of its sixties image created skeptical critics and societal dismay, Esalen helped institute many new practices involving psychoanalysis, psychotherapy, and humanistic and transpersonal psychologies. Carl Rogers' encounter groups and client-centered therapy, Fritz Perls' Gestalt therapy, Rollo May's human-development theory, and Abraham Maslow's self-actualization theory were practiced at Esalen in the sixties. Their presence at the Institute indicates the seriousness of its place in the study of human potential. In Anderson's words, "Humanistic psychology—by which I mean the intellectual movement identified with such people as Abraham Maslow, [Fritz] Perls, Carl Rogers, and Rollo May—seemed to me then (and still does) to contain an important part of the answer to what is tragically wrong with American life."[5]

While Will Schutz's T-groups, R. D. Laing's psychiatric techniques, Gregory Bateson's theory of mind, and Roberto Assagioli's psychosynthesis were also features at Esalen in the sixties and early seventies, the Institute is still offering seminars in Gestalt therapy, biofeedback, holistic health, and yoga. New are programs in the arts, anthropology, and philosophy. Seminars offered in 1993 included "Ecopsychology" (which was led by, among others, Theodore Roszak), "Zen Practice," and "Buddhism and Deep Ecology."[6] Much of the Institute's continuity and success can be attributed to its co-founders Murphy and Price (who died in 1985). They not only studied at the Academy of Asian Studies, but Murphy also spent sixteen months in the late 1950s practicing meditation in an ashram in India. Their mutual interest in Eastern philosophy has ensured its integration in Esalen programs from the beginning to the present.

Together, psychotherapy and Eastern thought have remained focal points in the Institute's prescription for treating the psychic imbalance fostered in the West. A perfect example of this prescription is articulated in the Esalen Book *Sacred Tradition and Present Need*, edited by Jacob Needleman and Dennis Lewis. After noting Esalen's decisive role "as a center and point of origin in the innovative approach to personal growth," Needleman argues that Eastern systems that had been previously "food for fantasy now seem to offer themselves as live options, each promising us a renewed and sacred relationship to our own being and to the cosmos that contains us." The emerging awareness of the relevance of these ancient traditions, he claims, marks for many "the present moment as the beginning of a new age." This awareness is not based on a "concern for the historical background," but on an application of what the traditions offer.[7]

Watts and his mentor, Daisetz Suzuki, are two of the scholars most responsible for making Eastern thought accessible to and popular in Western culture. While Suzuki promoted "The Awakening of a New Consciousness in Zen" (the title of his 1954 Eranos presentation), Watts's self-proclaimed philosophical quest became embedded in the aims of Esalen. In fact, it was during Watts's tenure (1952-1956) as the Academy of Asian Studies' director when Price (a former student of Watts's) and Murphy studied there. Besides speaking at the informal seminars held in various homes in Big Sur which resulted "in the founding of the Esalen Institute," Watts gave Esalen's first seminar in January, 1962.[8]

Watts's understanding of Eastern thought had a profound influence on Fritjof Capra, a friend and also a stalwart of Esalen's. Capra not only claims that Watts's work helped him more than anyone's in understanding the essence and the contemporary relevance of Eastern thought, he acknowledges that the source of success of *The Tao of Physics* "may well be that it is a book written in the tradition of Alan Watts." In 1977, four years after Watts held his last Esalen seminar, Capra instructed his first, in which he "explored parallels between modern physics and consciousness research"—an interest that Watts helped germinate and encouraged him to pursue.[9]

Watts and Capra share an enormous scope, a wide range of sources, and clear descriptions of the three paradigms. They both use Lao Tzu, Chuang Tzu, and Suzuki as major sources in their delineations of Earth wisdom; both point to the Socratic method, the Platonic and Christian separation of spirit and matter, and Newtonian mechanics as the backbone of the reason-as-virtue paradigm; and both integrate psychological theories of William James, Carl Jung, Ananda Coomaraswamy, and their Esalen colleagues Gregory Bateson and Abraham Maslow to restore the yin unconscious to yang consciousness. Both also implement ideas from Theodore Roszak, Joseph Needham, E. F. Schumaker, and systems theory to show how a reinstitution of intuitive powers could raise the aim of science and technology from mere quantitative functions toward an ecological end.

This final aim was among the themes discussed at the 1985 New Paradigm Symposium sponsored by Capra's Elmwood Institute and held at Esalen. According to Riane Eisler, the new-paradigm thinking at the symposium "was specifically described as 'postpatriarchal,' and the new epistemology was seen as representing a 'shift from domination and control of nature to cooperation and nonviolence.'"[10] This shift, Capra, Roszak, and Sam Keen maintain, began in the 1960s. All three agree that the counterculture not only supported ecological activism, the anti-war protest, and equal rights for minorities, women, and gays, it also put into practice a value system—immersed in Eastern philosophy and psychotherapy—that society has been and is being compelled to integrate.

Each of these thinkers acknowledges the role that Esalen has played in establishing this value system. In various surveys of new-paradigm scholarship's culminating phase, each scholar stresses the significance of the work of the following Esalen instructors: the psychology of Maslow, Perls, Rogers, Laing, Bateson; the Eastern mysticism of Huxley and Watts; and psychedelic teachings of Carlos Casteneda, John Lilly, Huxley, and Watts.[11]

All three also describe the influence that Esalen has had on them personally and/or on society at large. Capra and Keen, perhaps because of their friendships with key Esalen figures, tend to speak of Esalen personally. For instance, Capra (whose first visit to Esalen was for a Rock concert in the mid-sixties) discusses Esalen mostly in terms of his symposiums with Grof and Bateson, whereas Sam Keen—in a condescending tone—describes his first experience there (1968) in terms of the "sedate" nude bathing at the hot tubs, the flute music, incense, and the ocean. While Capra's discussion of Esalen is always congenial, Keen's is not. The latter admits his early bias against Esalen resulted from his "cherished prejudices" against the elitist, commercialized nature of meditation and Eastern spirituality in the West.[12] Although his long friendship with Michael Murphy, an avid meditation practitioner, softened this resistance, he has maintained serious questions concerning Esalen's motives, as he openly revealed in an address to several hundred people at a 1973 Esalen sponsored convention. In his talk, entitled "The Tyranny Game, or, How to Play Follow the Leader," he attacked the one-upmanship of the patient/client/disciple and therapist/guru relationship.[13] Despite these reservations, Keen affirms Esalen's role in directing countercultural energy toward the pursuit of establishing a new paradigm.

Theodore Roszak's evaluation of Esalen is particularly significant because it indicates the gradual sophistication of the Institute's aims. In *The Making of a Counter Culture*, he refers to Esalen only once, and then in a footnote, calling it the prototype of "hip spas" (hippies purportedly named it "the country club").[14] In his following three books, however, his estimation of Esalen becomes more and more positive. For instance, in *Where the Wasteland Ends: Politics and Transcendence in Postindustrial Society*, he states that "the wide-ranging Human Potential Movement encamped in its many Growth Centers across America" assumes a presence which mirrors the needs of society at large:

> Over the past generation, this 'eupsychian network' (as Abraham Maslow called it) has borrowed heavily on yogic, Taoist, and Tantric sources to propagate a variety of techniques for expanding personality. No question but that the promise of the movement is great. Yet there has often been a haunting ambiguity about its intentions, which I sense is only lately finding resolution.[15]

In *Unfinished Animal: The Aquarian Frontier and the Evolution of Consciousness*, he again smites the notion of weekend workshops, but adds that "such experiments are at least flirting with the emotional needs that once brought people to the traditional rites of religious passage, though how far a weekend of eclectic therapies will carry its participants is another question." Despite its weaknesses, Roszak calls Esalen the pioneer institution of "an astonishing number of techniques for exploring the full range of perception and consciousness; and from this has arisen a challenging new standard of psychic health and organic well-being which no school of psychiatry can any longer ignore without drastically limiting its understanding of human nature." Moreover, its "curriculum amounts to the most significant departure in Western education since the Renaissance: a brave effort to breakdown the verbal-cerebral monopoly over the personality."[16] By the time he wrote *Person/Planet: The Creative Disintegration of Industrial Society*, he was convinced that Esalen's inquiry into the "non-verbal Humanities" helped create a new "stream in educational change" by providing "an educational ideal that is justly proportioned to the whole human being–body, mind, and spirit."[17] Roszak suggests that the sophistication of Esalen's inquiry has evolved hand in hand with the sophistication of the counterculture's goals and influence.

Along with Roszak, Keen and Capra insist that what began as an inquiry into human potential has led to an awareness of human and planetary rights; or, in other words, new-paradigm scholarship has come of age. "The fantasy of radical change we played with in 1969," Keen claims, "has become a reality in 1990."[18] As Capra explains:

> The seventies brought consolidation of our views. The magic of the sixties faded; the initial excitement gave way to a period of focusing, digesting, integrating. Two new political movements [one involving the Greens and the other Czechoslavakian citizens], the ecology

> movement and the feminist movement, emerged during the seventies and together provided the much needed broad framework for our critique and alternative ideas. . . . in the seventies, we outlined the theoretical framework [of the cultural transformation]; in the eighties, we are fleshing it out.[19]

Still a participant in the "fleshing out" process, Esalen, like Eranos, attests to the fact that the new-paradigm tradition is composed of an array of interdisciplinary scholars committed to laying the foundations of a new value system, a system which—by integrating ecological and feminine principles—encourages a balanced worldview and a balanced self.

II

MODERN INDIVIDUAL VOICES

> The old doctrine of Egypt of the Secret of the Two Partners, the Mahayana of Voidness, Mutual Arising and the Flower Wreath, the Taoist of the complementarity of *yang* and *yin*, the Chinese Communist of interpermeation, and the Tantric lore of the presence within each being of all the gods and demons of all the storied heavens and hells: these, it would seem, variously turned and phrased, represent the one timeless doctrine of eternal life—the nectar of the fruit tree in the garden that Western man, or at least a notable number of his company, failed to eat.[1]

The new-paradigm message grew out of disparate voices calling for change, for a new way of understanding the self, for new forms of social interaction, and for a new interface with nature. From the poetical works of Nietzsche and Emerson to the psychology of Jung, Neumann, Eliade, Watts, and Campbell to the ecofeminism of Roszak, Capra, Keen, and Eisler, primal expressions of nature's balance have served as models for the pursued change. While the models supply a common philosophical framework, the scholars' individual reconstructions and applications of the particular expressions are invariably unique. Besides the diffusion of interdisciplinary lenses and languages, the primal expressions of nature's balance—which scholars use for their specific purposes—are also different. These differences continually extend the parameters of new-paradigm theory and ultimately confirm that the tradition has one central message.

The seven scholars whom I have chosen to survey as a representative group of the tradition use one or more of the following primal expressions of balance as (a) model(s): the Greek gods Dionysus and Apollo; the Indian gods Shiva and Vishnu; and the Chinese forces yin and yang. As the respective languages, myths, and religions demonstrate, each culture expresses its perceptions in diverse ways. For instance, Apollo and Dionysus often embody anthropomorphic characteristics; Vishnu and Shiva often possess polymorphic ones; and yang and yin represent cosmic forces. The notion of balance in each expression is correspondingly different. Interdependent cosmic principles, yin and yang unite in the Tao or the universal flow. The Indian gods merge metaphysically in Brahman, but similar to the Greek gods they are depicted with bodies, wills, and emotions–hence, their interdependence is most clearly interpreted in terms of personally opposed, yet complementary psychic forces. For example, in place of the dark, feminine force of yin which represents non-being and chaos, the male gods Dionysus and Shiva are often aggressive, destructive, and brutal.

The Tao represents the clearest and purest expression of balance simply because yin and yang exist in perfect harmony. From the Mother Earth and Father Sky worship to the oracular devices based on positive and negative principles to the flowering of classical philosophy, the Chinese observed, praised, and intuitively expressed the interplay of nature's polarities. The use of yin and yang as a new-paradigm model permeates the work of Alan Watts and Fritjof Capra. Watts, an established Orientalist, an ordained Episcopalian minister, and a self-acclaimed philosophical entertainer, used yin and yang to reinterpret Western myths, to revitalize the spirit within science, and to balance the unconscious with the ego. Capra, a high-energy physicist, has used yin and yang to explicate the similarities between Eastern mysticism and the new physics, the yin-integrated nature of systems theory, and the alternative value system of Greens and ecofeminists. As I shall argue, the Chinese primal expression of a cosmic, transpersonal balance–reconstructed by scholars such as Watts and Capra–supplies the new-paradigm tradition with its profoundest model.

Unlike yang and yin, Apollo and Dionysus, as well as Vishnu and Shiva share an antagonism. Originally identified as solar deities, Vishnu and Apollo promise their followers care for devotion; Shiva and Dionysus, on the other hand, are nature gods who offer their practitioners divinity through ecstatic union. The first set of gods, representing the personalized ego, determine order on earth from above; the latter, haunting mountains and forests, encourage civil abandonment and the release of the unconscious. According to Jung, it was Nietzsche's obsession with the mysterious, destructive impulse that ended in his insanity:

> He [Nietzsche] did not understand himself when he fell head first into the unutterable mystery and wanted to sing its praises to the dull, godforsaken masses. That was the reason for the bombastic language, the piling up of metaphors, the hymnlike raptures—all a vain attempt to catch the ear of a world which had sold its soul for a mass of disconnected facts. And he fell—tightrope-walker that he proclaimed himself to be—into depths far beyond himself. He did not know his way about in this world and was like a man possessed, one who could be handled only with the utmost caution.[2]

A philologist-turned-classicist, Nietzsche emphasized in his first book, *The Birth of Tragedy*, that Apollo and Dionysus "need each other," that they represented a balance achieved through the Apollonian control of Dionysian energies. However, in ensuing works, he left behind the concept of Apollonian control in favor of the Socratic drive, or Socratism, and built an increasingly dramatic case that the Dionysian propensity for fusion created the balance between the two. In short, the antagonism between the impulses became Nietzsche's foil because, in his quest of a purely Dionysian model, he lost sight of the balance.

Unlike Nietzsche, Sam Keen (a writer, lecturer, and former psychology of religion professor who regards himself as a Dionysian-oriented psychoanalyst), uses the primal Greek expression of balance to confront the West's psychic imbalance in terms of male and female virtues. In *Apology for Wonder* and *Life Maps* he describes the pathologies which result from an overemphasis of either the Apollonian or Dionysian impulses. As do Capra and Watts, Keen recognizes the balance of the polar forces as healthy and the imbalance as unhealthy.

Along with Dionysus, Shiva, and yin, new-paradigm scholarship has infused a fourth primal expression of the impulse which is suppressed in the West: the Mother Goddess or Great Mother. Although the Mother Goddess does not, in and of itself, constitute a model of balance, the notion of balance is, as

Erich Neumann clearly delineates, implicit. The balance of the Archetypal Feminine and Archetypal Masculine appears first, he claims, in the World Parents (the Father Sky and Mother Earth) or *hieros gamos* myths and rites of various prehistorical societies. Although the emphasis of the Masculine Archetype in the West has created the need to stress the reintegration of the Feminine Archetype, Neumann argues that this emphasis was a natural evolution in the history of consciousness. The evolution–from the prehistorical feminine unconscious to the masculine ego consciousness to the present reintegration of the unconscious–necessitates a swing from dominance of one to the other to a fully constituted balance of the two. This process is summarized in the conviction of Richard Tarnas (a director of Esalen for ten years):

> I believe that the West's restless inner development and incessantly innovative masculine ordering of reality has been gradually leading, in an immensely long dialectical movement, toward a reconciliation with the lost feminine unity, toward a profound and many-leveled marriage of the masculine and feminine, a triumphant and healing reunion. And I consider that much of the conflict and confusion of our own era reflects the fact that this evolutionary drama may now be reaching its climactic stages.[3]

In the context of this evolutionary drama as expressed in new-paradigm scholarship, the Mother Goddess or Feminine Archetype and the Dionysus/Shiva/yin impulse are interchangeable concepts. The interchangeability has an historical precedence. Male satellites of the Mother Goddess, Shiva and Dionysus represent her relationship to eroticism and ecstasy (kama/eros), androgyny, possession, dance and theater, creation and destruction, and the life force of animals and vegetation. As a number of new-paradigm scholars argue, the antagonistic qualities which differentiate Dionysus and Apollo as well as Shiva and Vishnu are explicable in terms of the Kurgan/Aryan invasions which resulted in the forced marriage of the planting societies' Mother Goddess to the hunting societies' warrior sky-gods. For instance, Riane Eisler uses archaeological findings to suggest that the diffusion of the symbols associated with the spread of the Mother Goddess, Shivan, and Dionysian cults (e.g., the bull and snake, the horns and erect phallus, his yoga position) is the result of a great Dravidian migration from India to Portugal circa 6,000 B.C.; and that waves of Northern, sky-god worshipping, nomadic hunters/warriors invaded, conquered, and ultimately destroyed the peaceful, nonhierarchical way of life of the agricultural, matrilineal, Mother Goddess-worshipping societies of prehistory.

In terms of the new-paradigm theme, scholars such as Eisler, Neumann, Jung, Campbell, and Roszak describe the Great Mother, Shiva, and Dionysus as archetypal expressions of humankind's originally harmonious relationship with nature. The worship of the goddess and gods was a natural response to the awareness of the unity between the self and the cosmos. The scholars have termed this awareness "Earth Wisdom," a communication with nature foreign to Western civilization and sacred to primal peoples. Theodore Roszak, a cultural historian who assimilates Jung's and Neumann's work with the archetype, uses the Mother Goddess, Dionysus, and Shiva to expose the evils of technocracy, to reveal the mythology and philosophy behind the 1960s revolution, to fuel his ecofeminist perspective, and to convey how Earth wisdom provides a model for the cultural transformation theory.

Clearly, the thematic foci, perspectives, and fields of new-paradigm scholars vary greatly. However, the awareness of life's interrelatedness and a deep reverence for nature's balance unites their messages. The focal point of this unity is the recognition that the Dionysus/Shiva/yin or Mother Goddess impulse represents dark, instinctive, emotional, mysterious, feminine, synthesizing, and intuitive principles and that Apollo/Vishnu/yang or the Father-sky impulse reflects light, civilizing, intellectual, moralizing, masculine, discriminating, and rational ones. The message corresponding to the recognition is that the West needs to reintegrate the former with the latter. In Capra's words, "What we need, then, is a new 'paradigm'—a new vision of reality, a fundamental change in our thoughts, perceptions and values."[4] The following chronologically arranged survey of seven scholars—Friedrich Nietzsche, Erich Neumann, Alan Watts, Theodore Roszak, Sam Keen, Fritjof Capra, and Riane Eisler—exemplifies the new-paradigm tradition's three periods, the wide range of inquiries, the various reconstructions of primal expressions, and the united message.

4

The Antipatriarchal Nature of Friedrich Nietzsche's Masculine *Übermensch*

> From that height of joy where man feels himself to be altogether a deified form and a self-justification of nature, down to the joy of healthy peasants and healthy half-human animals, this whole, long, tremendous light and color scale of happiness, the Greeks, not without the grateful shudder of him who is initiated into a mystery, not without much caution and pious silence, called by the divine name: *Dionysus*. What do any latter-day men, the children of a fragmentary, multifarious, sick, strange age, know of the *range* of Greek happiness; what *could* they know of it! Whence would the slaves of "modern ideas" derive a right to Dionysian festivals![1]

Friedrich Nietzsche constantly expresses his hatred for what he considers to be his pathologically bourgeois society. "Morality in Europe today," he claims in *Beyond Good and Evil*, "is herd-instinct Morality."[2] Consistently stressing that the herd morality has been sustained in the West through Greek philosophy, Christianity, and science, Nietzsche argues in *Genealogy of Morals* that the morality originated with masses subject to a ruling class. Bred in humility and helplessness, the slave class valued pity, moderation, and security over courage, adventure, and initiative. Nietzsche bluntly states several times that the Jewish tradition epitomized the origin and development of the slave or herd morality. Understandably, in the face of the resurgent interest in his work, vociferous protests have been raised against his prejudices. The darkest accusation regarding Nietzsche involves the association of his philosophy with the politics of Hitler's Third Reich.

Although Jews, Christians, Greek philosophers, and scientists were subjects of Nietzsche's attack, no group incurred more wrath than women. Nietzsche apparently took pleasure in addressing women in a condescending tone. Amidst an onslaught on femininity in *Beyond Good and Evil*, Nietzsche concludes:

> Woman wants to become self-reliant–and for that reason she is beginning to enlighten men about "woman as such": *this* is one of the worst developments of the general *uglification* of Europe. For what must these clumsy attempts of women at scientific self-exposure bring to light! Woman has much reason for shame; so much pedantry, superficiality, schoolmarmishness, petty presumption, petty licentiousness and immodesty lie concealed in woman–one only needs to study her behavior with children!–and so far all this was at bottom best repressed and kept under control by *fear* of man. . . . Even now female voices are heard which–holy Aristophanes!–are frightening: they threaten with medical explicitness what woman *wants* from man, first and last. Is it not in the worst taste when woman sets about becoming scientific that way?[3]

In "Friedrich Nietzsche/Woman De-Feminized," Betty and Theodore Roszak argue that it is typical of Nietzsche to associate "feminism with socialism, pacifism, and with democratic values generally. Thus we have a broadside rejection of everything on the social scene that challenged the privileges of Europe's militaristic elites."[4]

Why, then, with all the prejudices apparent in his writings, has there been a revival of Nietzsche's work? In "Aristophanes, Nietzsche, and the Death of Tragedy," Rainer Friedrich insists that the new interest exists because of the recognition of Nietzsche's work as a classicist and because "current intellectual fashions"–such as "New Sensibility, Post-Modernism, Post-structuralist Freudianism, Übermensch-Socialism" and other movements associated with "the New Irrationalism"–encourage the "*Nietzsche Redivivus*."[5] The value of Nietzsche's work as a classicist continues to be a subject of debate; however, his holistic writing style certainly explains part of the new fascination with Nietzsche. Deconstructionists, for example, have described Nietzsche's writing as creatively unstructured and purposely relative to the reader's perspective and perceptions. Nietzsche's "meaning," Jacques Derrida explains in *Writing and Difference*, is indivisible from his affirmation "of a world of signs without fault, without truth, and without origin which is offered to an active interpretation."[6] Or, as Christoper Norris asserts in *Deconstruction: Theory and Practice*, Nietzsche introduces a "style of philosophic writing which remains intensely skeptical of all claims to truth–its own included–and which thus opens up the possibility of liberating thought from its age-old conceptual limits."[7]

Whether or not Nietzsche aimed his style at such a liberation, the content of his philosophy was aimed most assuredly at liberating society from what he considered to be its age-old, worn-out, life-denying values–as alone the following titles to his books indicate: *Beyond Good and Evil: A Prelude to a Philosophy of the Future*, *Twighlight of the Idols*, and *The Antichrist*. More than anything else, this attempt, linked to his vision of an ideal human who balances the opposing yet complementary psychological principles characteristic of the human mind, accounts for Nietzsche's contemporary relevance.

Nietzsche codified the notion of a psychological balance in terms of Apollonian and Dionysian impulses in *The Birth of Tragedy*. The book–despite numerous attacks–has endured as a scholarly focal point in the study of the classical mind. Ulrich Wilamowitz-Moellendorf, Nietzsche's contemporary, completely discredited the book, calling it the product of "ignorance and lack of love of truth."[8] In *An Attempt at a Self-Criticism*, Nietzsche describes *Birth* as "badly written, ponderous, embarrassing, image-mad and image-confused."[9] To be sure, as Walter Burkert explains, Nietzsche's delineation of Apollo's and Dionysus' relationship often strays from the heritage of both gods.

However vaguely, Nietzsche does supply an historical context while explaining how the Apollonian and Dionysian impulses fluctuated throughout four periods of Greek culture. He refers to the first period of "the older Hellenic history" as the Homeric world which–guided by the strain for Olympian order–"developed under the sway of the Apollonian impulse to beauty." The second period marks the influx of the Dionysian via the development of proto-tragedy by, among others, Pindar. The third period, a reaction to the merger of the other two, culminated in "the austere majesty of Doric art and the Doric view of the world" (which for Nietzsche represented a "military encampment of the Apollonian"). The "climax and aim of these artistic impulses" occurred in the fourth and final period. "And here the sublime and celebrated art of *Attic tragedy* and the dramatic dithyramb presents itself as the common goal of both these tendencies whose mysterious union, after many and long precursory struggles, found glorious consummation. . . ."[10]

Nietzsche depicts this consummation as unfolding from the triumph of the dithyrambic chorus to the crowning of the masked Dionysian heroes, Prometheus and Oedipus. In other words, he claims that tragedy crystalized in the merger of the intoxicating principles of the Dionysian chorus with the dramatic imagery and the rational voice of Apollonian structure; that "until Euripides, Dionysus never ceased to be the tragic hero; and that all the celebrated figures of the Greek stage–Prometheus, Oedipus, etc.–are mere masks of the original hero, Dionysus." The result of Dionsysian energies being directed by Apollonian order meant, first, that Dionysus spoke the Apollo's language, or that the satyr "folk song" evolved into drama; and secondly, that "Apollo finally [learned] the language of Dionysus," or that the sole theme of the early performances of the suffering and ecstasy of Dionysus were given precise and lucid expression in Attic tragedy. Amidst the ways in which Nietzsche suggests that the balance is achieved in the trilogies of Aeschylus and Sophocles, one stands clear: Prometheus and Oedipus undergo a Dionysian-like fate ordained by the Olympian system, but eventually they transcend their suffering and reconcile with the system while individually becoming divine.[11]

Despite his unconventional method as a classicist and his uncomprimising writing style, Nietzsche opened new ways of understanding the evolution of the ancient Greek mind, as Joseph Campbell acknowledges:

> Friedrich Nietzsche was the first, I believe, to recognize the force in the Greek heritage of an interplay of two mythologies: the pre-Homeric Bronze Age heritage of the peasantry, in which release from the yoke of individuality was achieved through group rites inducing rapture; and the Olympian mythology of measure and humanistic self-knowledge that is epitomized for us in Classical art. The glory of the Greek tragic

view, he perceived, lay in its recognition of the mutuality of these two orders of spirituality, neither of which alone offers more than a partial experience of human worth.[12]

While Nietzsche's recognition of the clash and synthesis of the two cultures ensured him a place in classical studies, his theory regarding human worth has captured the attention of many new-paradigm scholars, from Carl Jung to Sam Keen. What makes his delineation of the four periods of Greek culture so significant is his description of how the relationship between the Apollonian principle of light, reason, control, and order and the dark, irrational, mysterious principle of Dionysus sways through Greek culture in "perpetual strife with only periodic reconciliations," a process which allows them to "continually incite each other to new and more powerful births."[13] In other words, Nietzsche decribes in Greek culture a mythological expression of aesthetic impulses and, more generally, psychological principles which, when balanced, constitute full human worth.

Nietzsche compares Apollonian consciousness to dreams because it creates the "illusion" of order which makes things intelligible as well as beautiful, and Dionysian instinct to "intoxication" because it possesses nature's darker, mysterious, ecstatic tendencies. He insists that Apollo without Dionysus remains unaware of nature's power and out of touch with the extreme pleasures and pains of life; and Dionysus without Apollo lacks the reason or purpose to control or balance creative energies. Accordingly, Apollo and Dionysus, the rational principle of individuation and the emotional urge for fusion or immersion of self in nature, need each other.

Beginning with the advent of the Olympian spirit and ending with the sacrifice of the spirit to the myth of scientific truth, Nietzsche discusses ways in which Western morality has cultivated obsessively the Apollonian principle and suppressed the Dionysian. He argues, very simply, that the Socratic/scientific eulogy of reason along with Christianity's sacred logos banished the Dionysian impulse from acceptable human endeavor.

The argument begins in *Birth* with the claim that Euripides' dramatic principle "to be beautiful everything must be intelligible" is the counterpart to the Socratic dictum "knowledge is virtue." Nietzsche feels that the rational spirit initiated by Socrates was a momentous perversity—"there is, to be sure, a profound *illusion* that first saw the light of the world in the person of Socrates: the unshakable faith that thought, using the thread of causality, can penetrate the deepest abysses of being, and that thought is capable not only of knowing being but even of *correcting* it."[14] By assuming that reason is capable of improving whatever it touches, Socrates helped science to create and sustain its own myth, namely, that the only proper relationship to life rests in the attempt to understand and to better it. This Apollonian "urge to correct" has cultivated a rational idealism in the West that has profaned humankind's connection to nature.

By setting his sights on the "heavenly" aspirations of reason, Western man has constructed what Nietzsche regards as a most treacherous concept, the *deus ex machina*. Armed with the belief that behind beauty and reason stands an "ultimate logician," Greek philosophers along with Christians and scientists have sealed and kept sealed Dionysus' tomb. The culminating concept of a tradition which began with Anaxagoras' *nous* (the divine mind that created order out of chaos), the *deus ex machina* was crowned by Descartes—who "could prove the reality of the empirical world by virtue of an appeal to God's truthfulness and inability to tell lies." This assumption epitomized for Nietzsche the rationalistic conceit which demonized Dionysus and profaned the ecstatic realm, wherein "all of the gulfs between man and man are overcome by an overwhelming feeling of oneness which leads back to the heart of nature."[15]

Nietzsche considers Christian morality to be an unfortunate extension of the Socratic virtue-as-knowledge ideal. "Not the 'moral corruption' of antiquity, but precisely its *moralization* is the prerequisite through which alone Christianity could become master of it. Moral fanaticism . . . destroyed paganism, by revaluing its values and poisoning its innocence."[16] Accordingly, the Christian belief in salvation is but another manifestation of the West's hostile-to-life and instinct-denying attitude:

> Dionysus versus the "Crucified": there you have the antithesis. It is *not* a difference in regard to their martyrdom—it is a difference in the meaning of it . . . whether a Christian meaning or a tragic meaning. In the former case, it is supposed to be the path to a holy existence; in the latter case, being is counted as *holy enough* to justify even a monstrous amount of suffering. . . . The god on the cross is a curse on life, a signpost to seek redemption from life; Dionysus cut to pieces is a *promise* of life: it will be eternally reborn and return again from destruction.[17]

The turning away from life, Nietzsche argues, has been an institutionalized preoccupation of Western society. From the degradation of the body and nature through the vehicle of logos to science's manipulative, measuring, correcting attitude toward nature, the evolution of Western thought has climaxed in a spiritual crisis. The way out of the modern dilemma is to revitalize the Dionysian impulse, a process that he characterizes in his vision of the new man, the *Übermensch* or Overman.

The qualities of Nietzsche's Overman are predominantly masculine. He not only considers the Roman embodiment of fortitude, strength, and power to be the epitome of master morality, Nietzsche praises the brutality of the Aryans. Immersed in patriarchal traits and values, Nietzsche's ideal man is "beyond good and evil, the master of his virtues, he that is overrich in will."[18] Or, "Man is beast and superbeast; the higher man is inhuman and superhuman . . ."[19] Pity, gentleness, meekness, and other such emotions or traits he regards as "womanish" signs of weakness. Obviously, Nietzsche's depiction of a balanced self lacks a feminine principle. Although he suggests that the mystical tendency of Dionysus lies "open to the Mothers of Being" (a phrase he borrowed from Goethe) and that humans are impelled to exist by virtue of the "primordial mother," he does not regard Dionysian tendencies as emanating from a feminine source. In fact, Nietzsche contends that women are sick and inconstant, always conspiring to weaken the strength and power of men.[20]

What is lacking, then, in Nietzsche's concept of Dionysus/Zarathustra/*Übermensch*, or his model of the ideal man, is the Archetypal Feminine. He either does not recognize or fails to admit that Dionysus was originally a god of women. In terms of his cult, Dionysus offered women the means to meet in a religiously meaningful sense outside of the auspices of patriarchal control–or, as Bachofen asserts, "Dionysus is a woman's god in the fullest sense of the word, the source of all woman's sensual and transcendent hopes, the center of her whole existence. It was to women that he was first revealed in his glory, and it was women who propagated his cult and brought about its triumph."[21] In myth, as Walter Otto relates, the original world of Dionysus comprises women. They awaken, save, nurture, await, accompany, and serve him. They are also the first to succumb to his possessive powers.[22]

Despite Nietzsche's obsession with masculinity and condemnation of femininity, the emergence of his masculine Dionysus/Zarathustra/*Übermensch* would involve necessarily a dissolution of the patriarchal value system. Everything the Übermensch represents–the dark, intuitive, mysterious, and unconscious aspects of the psyche–is antipatriarchal. He not only revolts against set value systems, he embraces in nature the ultimate experiences of suffering and ecstasy. In terms which resound the feminine principle, Nietzsche describes both the nature and value of the Dionysian impulse as "an urge to unity, a reaching out beyond personality, the everyday, society, reality, across the abyss of transitoriness; a passionate-painful overflowing into darker, fuller, more floating states; an ecstatic affirmation of the total character of life . . . ."[23]

Beyond its pro-patriarchal, anti-Semitic and anti-feminist elements, Friedrich Nietzsche's philosophy contains the seeds of new-paradigm thinking. Repulsed by the West's "desanctification" of instinct, ecstasy, and nature, Nietzsche condemns Socratic, Christian, and scientific decadence and preaches a "transvaluation of values beyond good and evil." Although his version of the Dionysian impulse ignores the feminine aspects which the tradition accords it, his original imperative that the West must learn to balance the polar principles holds the key to understanding his contemporary relevance.

5

Erich Neumann's Theory of the Evolving Psyche: From the Masculine Ego to the Archetypal Feminine

> The Great Goddess . . . is the incarnation of the Feminine Self that unfolds in the history of mankind as in the history of every individual woman; its reality determines individual as well as collective life. This archetypal psychical world which is encompassed in the multiple forms of the Great Goddess is the underlying power that even today . . . determines the psychic history of modern man and modern woman.[1]

Erich Neumann casts his psychological/mythological theory in the form of a prophecy: by virtue of an ever-expanding collective psyche, human consciousness has evolved to a point where a shift which will diminish the powers of personal ego consciousness and integrate the transpersonal unconscious is inevitable. The inevitability of this shift can be demonstrated, Neumann avers, through an analysis of the significance of myth for modern Western "man" and the way it has mirrored the growth of his personality.[2] By tracing the history of the evolution of human consciousness through succeeding stages of mythological archetypes, Neumann shows that the masculinization of consciousness and the resulting emancipation of the ego as portrayed in the hero's journey and transformation–which represents a state of awareness that has dominated Western civilization–is giving way to a reintegration of the feminine unconscious as portrayed through the uroboros (the snake biting its tail) and Great Mother archetypes. He spells out his theoretical vision in *The Origins and History of Consciousness* and *The Great Mother: An Analysis of the Archetype*.

In *Origins*, which Jung suggests contains "conclusions and insights which are among the most important ever to be reached in this field," Neumann maintains that creation myths involving the uroboros and the World Egg represent the pre-ego unconscious, a state wherein the beginning is portrayed in its "perfection" and "wholeness." Both the cyclical uroboros and the spherical World Egg symbolize the "source situation," or being without beginning or end, before space or time, without conflict or opposites:

> . . . the uroboros, the circular snake biting its tail, is the symbol of the psychic state of the beginning, of the original situation, in which man's consciousness and ego were still small and undeveloped. As symbol of the origin and of the opposites contained in it, the uroboros is the "Great Round," in which positive and negative, male and female, elements of consciousness, elements hostile to consciousness, and unconscious elements are intermingled. In this sense the uroboros is also a symbol of a state in which chaos, the unconscious, and the psyche as a whole were undifferentiated–and which is experienced by the ego as a borderline state.[3]

The only aspect of the ego symbolized here is light, the "dawn state" which "functions as a transpersonal factor that was there as a psychic stage of being before the formation of an ego." The ego is present, but only as an embryonic awareness of the eternal round, which encompasses the reality of the ego and everything else in an "infinite unity and unimaged wholeness . . . which even our present-day consciousness can only understand as paradoxes, precisely because it cannot grasp them."[4]

The next stage, represented by the Great Mother (the goddess of opposites), marks the ego's first awareness of itself. The ambivalent universe–governed by the Terrible Mother of earthquakes, floods, plagues, famines, and death, and the Good Mother of life, abundance, happiness, and grace–reflects the ego consciousness' recognition of pain and pleasure. Despite this awareness, the ego remains under the dominance of the Great Mother: "In childhood and early youth, both mankind and the individual must come to grips with the Mother archetype, who is the terrible, devouring Mother," the aspect of the Archetypal Feminine which the youth or ego-to-be must confront and conquer. Only with the separation of the World Parents, which creates the principle of opposites, does the ego consciousness first assert itself. With the separation of the masculine-light-day-heaven from the feminine-dark-night-earth, the suddenly volitional ego is able to make the instinctual Great Mother-unconscious a content of consciousness. In the light of day, the self-orienting consciousness, the "I," emerges and recognizes its "manly opposition to the feminine unconscious."[5]

The adolescent ego consciousness, despite its liberation, feels powerless, uncertain, and lonely because of its recognition of the separation of opposites—such as the sacred and profane, subject and object, and self and nature. Only with the birth of the hero, which represents the masculinization of consciousness and the true liberation of the ego, does a new phase of myth and human personality come into being. After surviving the pains of birth and being dominated by the uroboros/Great Mother, the hero-ego kills the Goddess-protecting dragon and gains control of the unconscious. This feat also includes the slaying of the Great Mother's male satellites, the child-eating father figures or phallic Earth Fathers, which ensures an eternal affiliation with the Good Father of sky and light. This victory culminates in the hero's reward: "the treasure hard to attain"—an archetypal symbol such as a virgin, magic ring or weapon, etc.—which represents his personal achievement as a new patriarchal force. The victory, Neumann suggests, symbolizes a new stage in human consciousness evolution:

> With the hero myth we enter upon a new phase of stadial development. . . . This means . . . not only that man's ego consciousness has achieved independence, but that his total personality has detached itself from the natural context of the surrounding world and the unconscious. Although the separation of the World Parents is, strictly speaking, an integral part of the hero myth, the developments which, at that stage, could only be represented in cosmic symbols now enter the phase of humanization and personality formation. Thus the hero is the archetypal forerunner of mankind in general. His fate is the pattern in accordance with which the masses of humanity must live, and always have lived, however haltingly and distantly; and however short of the ideal man they have fallen, the stages of the hero myth have become constituent elements in the personal development of every individual.[6]

Following the destruction of the dragon, or the guardian of the Terrible Mother, the hero engages in a sacred marriage with the virgin, the prisoner or anima, freed from the dragon's grip. The marriage symbolizes a reunion of the creative fertility power once associated with the World Parents, but now the ego consciousness has gained control of the source situation and, in so doing, has entered adulthood. By killing the dragon, the hero is initiated and reborn into the divine mystery as the "son of the godhead, a spiritual being" who has "achieved 'higher' manhood. Only after this metamorphosis is the ego capable of becoming a vehicle of culture and an adult member of society."[7]

Neumann distinguishes between three directions of personality development resulting from the hero's victory: extraverted outward adaptation, based on a militant-hero type; introverted inward adaptation, based on a culture-hero type; and centroverted synthetic adaptation, based on a self-realized hero type. The first two have been crowned by modern man as the warrior and the savior, scientist and poet, athlete and artist, political leader and inventor. The centroverted individual, whose tendency to self-actualization proceeds within the psyche itself, has as his primary goal or treasure the transformation of personality. Like the two traditional hero types, the transformed personality has grown by consolidating the ego while protecting it from the perils of the world and by stabilizing consciousness while protecting it from the perils of the soul. However, unlike the other two (who have been around for centuries), the centroverted hero is only now reaching beyond its infant stage. Representing the assimilation of the unconscious into consciousness, the centroverted individual marks the shift from the ego to the self and signifies the latest stage in the evolution of human consciousness. In short, centroversion is the process whereby the ego recognizes the whole self and willingly submits part of its domain to the instincts of the libido and the unconscious in general—a phenomenon which will decide the fate of both the individual and humankind:

> The civilization that is about to be born will be human civilization in a far higher sense than any has ever been before, as it will have overcome important social, national, and racial limitations. These are not fantastic pipe dreams, but hard facts. . . . The turning of the mind from the conscious to the unconscious, the responsible *rapprochement* of the

human consciousness with the powers of the collective psyche, that is the task of the future.[8]

In *The Great Mother,* which Neumann states "may be regarded wholly as a presentation of the Eranos archive," the author amplifies depth psychology's interpretation of the Mother Goddess archetype. He also expands his theme developed in *Origins*: through centroversion, Western civilization must balance its "one-sidedly patriarchal development of the male intellectual conscious" with "the feminine world. . . . Only then will the individual human being be able to develop the psychic wholeness that is urgently needed if Western man is to face the dangers that threaten his existence from within and without."[9]

Neumann insists that the "pure spirit" concept formulated in the "Apollonian-Platonic and Jewish-Christian" tradition is responsible for the schism between reason and intuition, ego and libido, consciousness and the unconscious in the modern Western psyche. Represented in the hero's conquest, the transcendence of the spirit from the body—epitomized in the claim "I and the Father are One"—has encouraged the West's repression of the unconscious which, in turn, has nearly obliterated the symbols, myths, rites, and worship of balance associated with the Mother Goddess.

The central symbol of the Mother Goddess, the vessel, not only corresponds to the womb, the earth, and the dark mystery, it represents the creative powers of transformation and regeneration. While this symbol has retained a meaningful place in the patriarchal psyche of the West, its representation has been demonized. In place of harmony, ecstasy, and nature, the ego consciousness has transmuted the realm of the Mother Goddess with notions such as evil, sex, and hell. The reintegration of the Great Mother, an evolutionary process which Neumann insists is now taking place, will reinstitute the sacredness of the body, the earth, and the Archetypal Feminine. Through centroversion, the original unity of the World Parents, the balance of self and ego, and the return of the Good Mother will be achieved individually and collectively. Because "the Feminine contains opposites, and the world actually lives because it combines earth and heaven, night and day, death and life," the truth of her symbols demands recognition.[10] As such, the Great Goddess symbolizes "everything we have attempted to represent as the archetypal unity and multiplicity of the feminine nature."[11]

While Neumann is convinced of the need to integrate the ecstatic, instinct-freeing power of the Archetypal Feminine (which he claims is exemplified in Dionysus and Shiva), he is careful to warn of its possessive and even destructive potential and the danger of losing the ego to the unconscious. Just as the evolution of the psyche from the source situation to the dominance of the male ego contains tensions, uncertainties, and dangers, the reintegration of the Archetypal Feminine necessitates a struggle to resolve the extreme tension between the established ego and the emerging balanced self. The shift toward a union of the conscious and the unconscious in the individual and collective psyche will be a difficult, painful, yet enlightening process.

6

Alan Watts's Word on Myths of Polarity: Power to Women, Nature, and the Left Hand of God

> . . . the differences of the world are not isolated objects encountering one another in conflict, but expressions of polarity. Opposites and differences have something between them, like the two faces of a coin; they do not meet as total strangers. When this relativity of things is seen very strongly, its appropriate effect is love rather than hate or fear.[1]

Alan Watts began studying Eastern philosophy at a very young age. A convert to Buddhism at fifteen, he credits much of his early education to Christmas Humphreys, a former Theosophist and the founder of the Buddhist Lodge in London–where Watts claims to have begun his philosophical explorations. It was his education in Eastern thought and his flair for the dramatic which helped establish him as a hero of the beat generation. An authority on consciousness-changing drugs as well as a popularizer of "the Spirit of Zen" in the 1960s, Watts has contributed greatly to the social awareness of the need to establish a new paradigm. His work, consisting of over twenty books and a plethora of articles, begins with the premise that Western society needs to adopt a new understanding of humankind's relationship to nature and ends with the conclusion that the key to this understanding is the recognition that "the art of life is not seen as holding to yang and banishing yin, but as keeping the two in balance, because there cannot be one without the other."[2] Incessantly, Watts contends that a Western world reinstatement of yin values holds the key to survival.

He espouses his theme through four interrelated processes: a reinterpretation of the mythology regarding the relationship between the Christian God and the Devil; a reevaluation of Western man's relationship with nature and woman; a refocusing of the aims and methods of science and technology; and the use of Taoism as a model to re-balance Western thinking. Each of these processes, Watts insists, necessitates a reevaluation of the significance of the ego, control, and reason through a re-identification with the unconscious and intuition.

Watts depicts the Christian split between divine spirit and profane nature (the realm of the Devil) as the focal point of the West's yang-dominated value system. The God of ecclesiastical imagery, the Father-Spirit in the sky, author of logos and enemy of evil, governs the universe with a holy vengeance. The source of evil, the most sinister and malicious demon ever imagined, is the Devil, whose "popular form is simply that of the god Pan—the lusty spirit of earth and fertility, the genius of natural beauty [which he uses to corrupt and capture humans]. Hell, his domain, lies downward in the heart of the earth, where all is dark, inward, and unconscious as distinct from the bright heavens above."[3] This absolute dichotomy enforces the Christian aim to transcend the instincts of the body and to escape death through salvation.

Emphasizing the necessary interdependence between polar forces in all myths (particularly in *The Two Hands of God: The Myths of Polarity*), Watts attempts to bridge the chasm between the Christian God and the Devil by reinterpreting them as necessary companions whose antagonism is tempered by a mutual sympathy. This interpretation, which provides an outlet for the ecstatic, unconscious, dark side of being human, is revealed in "the very fact that the name of the angel of evil is Lucifer, the light-bearer," which "suggests that there might be something formative and creative in becoming conscious of one's own evil principle, or dark side, or innate rascality." Hence, Watts ordains it as the duty of every individual to, "as Jung would say, integrate the evil one":

> The sensation of being threatened, spiritually, by a weirdly alien and incalculable power of malice is, above all, a symptom of unconsciousness—of man's alienation from himself. Furthermore, inasmuch as he is unconscious of the Devil as his own image, he is the more apt to vent upon his fellows his fear of and fury at this disowned aspect of himself.

> This is why the acceptance of the Devil in and as oneself is a moral obligation.[4]

The split between God and the Devil is, then, psychologically explicable. Because of an over-developed ego, Westerners have been conditioned to regard consciousness as good and the unconscious as evil. Hence, the problem for God (the ego of the universe) becomes the problem for the human ego. "The Devil is God's unconsciously produced shadow. Naturally, God is not allowed to be responsible for the origin of evil, for the connection between the two lies in the unconscious."[5] Just as God found it necessary to condemn the Devil to the confines of the earth's center, humans have imprisoned the unconscious.

This imprisonment not only precludes man from a harmonious relationship with nature and his own instincts, but also with woman, simply because there has always been a correlation between man's regard for nature and man's regard for woman. Women, the traditionally accepted agents of sexual desire, have been regarded as *objects* to be tamed and controlled.

The split between nature and spirit has not only adulterated man's understanding of instinct and his relationship with woman, but has encouraged the scientific attitude to dominate and control nature. "God," declares Watts, "is actually conceived as a set of principles–principles of morality and reason, of science and art. His love tempered with justice is likewise principled, since it is willed love rather than felt love, the masculine Logos rather than the feminine Eros."[6] With the invention of logos, "what is impossible and unimaginable in nature is possible in idea–as that the positive may be separated permanently from polarity with the negative, and joy from interdependence with sorrow. In short, purely verbal possiblity is considered as having a higher reality than physical possibility."[7] Language, or at least the conventional linear use of it, has helped invoke the West's complete trust in the efficacy and authority of logos:

> There are two principal ways in which the power of the Word assists this [Western] type of consciousness. The first is that words provide a notation for a style of consciousness based on noticing. . . . It is to use the mind like a spotlight, illuminating the world bit by bit–keeping the bits organized and classified by the system of tags or pigeonholes which

words provide. The second is that words give us a model or symbol of the world which is much easier to understand than the world itself.[8]

By using reason to break down phenomena into parts, to separate events in terms of cause and effect, and to control the environment through an ever-expanding body of knowledge, Western man has found a way to transcend and reign over nature. Technology has become a means of exploiting nature. Through furious attempts to achieve yang dominance, "we have been interfering with a complex system of relationships which we do not understand, and the more we study its details, the more it eludes us by revealing still more details to study."[9] Despite the scientist's dependence on intuition to understand complex systems of relationships, "he does not trust it. He must always stop to check intuitive insight with the thin bright beam of analytical thought."[10]

Despite this prejudice, scientists are being forced to intuitively recognize that separations between mind and matter as well as subject and object are mere conventions of language; that nature's "patterns are not determinative but descriptive. This is a fundamental revolution in the philosophy of science which has hardly reached the general public and which has still but barely affected some of the special sciences."[11] This revolution sprang from the need to view the relationship between nature and the self from the "inside," where words, categories, and measurements are recognized as external facts and not internal truths. The consequences of the revolution will be nothing short of a new paradigm which encourages the cultivation of intuition and accords nature the meaning it richly deserves. Giving science a heart (a metaphor both Watts and Capra use) changes its aims and methods.

The re-identification with nature from the "inside" is expressed most poignantly in Taoism. The Chinese regard nature as organic and perfect, whereas Westerners, who erroneously understand nature as blind and matter as inert, regard it as mechanical and imperfect. Unlike the nature-suppressing belief system practiced in Christianity and the quantitative approach of Western science, the Taoist philosophy of nature is not a mere theoretical system; rather, it "is primarily a way of life in which the original sense of the seamless unity of nature is restored without the loss of individual consciousness."[12] The restoration of this unity, then, hinges upon the recognition of nature's balance:

> At the very roots of Chinese thinking and feeling there lies the principle of polarity, which is not to be confused with the ideas of opposition or conflict. In the metaphors of other cultures, light is at war with darkness, life with death, good with evil, and the positive with the negative, and thus idealism to cultivate the former and be rid of the latter flourishes throughout much of the world. To the traditional way of Chinese thinking, this is as incomprehensible as an electric current without both positive and negative poles, for polarity is the principle that + and -, north and south, are different aspects of one and the same system, and that the disappearance of either one of them would be the disappearance of the system.[13]

The West's assimilation of the Taoist model of balance would require a revision of traditional common sense, particularly in regards to the pursuit of the ideal good and pleasure and to the elimination of evil and the painful. Perhaps the most significant and difficult concept for Westerners to understand is the Taoist notion of nature's order. This order is exemplified in the Chinese word for nature: *tzu-jan*, which literally means "of itself so," or, less equivocally, "spontaneity." Unlike the forced order imposed by a transcendent Creator or the captured order of scientifically discovered laws, the spontaneous order as described in Taoist philosophy may be experienced but not conceived, intuited but not classified, sensed but not articulated. This nonrepetitive, asymmetrical order is neither created nor planned, it simply is. It defies rational explication because it dissolves all notions of internal and external components, of cause and effect. On the basis of concomitant properties such as spontaneity and relativity, the Chinese notion of order is ineffably harmonious: "Because of the mutual interdependence of all beings, they will harmonize if left alone and not forced into conformity with some arbitrary, artificial, and abstract notion of order, and this harmony will emerge *tzu-jan*, of itself, without external compulsion."[14]

According to Watts, just as the concepts of relativity and spontaneity have been assimilated by physicists to supply a more comprehensive worldview than the Newtonian one, the realm of moral inquiry must also incorporate the same concepts in order to transcend the West's traditionally mechanical, good-versus-evil value system. "The senses, feelings, and thoughts," Watts asserts, "must be allowed to be spontaneous (*tzu-jan*) in the faith that they will then order themselves harmoniously."[15] He explains that the Taoists describe spontaneous action, a quality of the Tao manifest in *tzu-jan*, in terms of "*wu-wei*," which is translated often as inaction but actually means not acting in discord with nature. As the Tao balances yin and yang through *wu-wei*, the human being balances his/her life by not "trying" to do anything. Rather, one simply allows oneself to react with, not against, the environment, accepting freely the simultaneous relationship between the outer stimuli and the inner response. "Spontaneity is, after all, total sincerity–the whole being involved in the act without the slightest reservation."[16]

In sum, the problems associated with the attempts to control nature, instinct, and the mind through external compulsion are, Watts insists, problems of the ego: "The realization that nature is ordered organically rather than politically, that it is a field of relationships rather than a collection of things, requires an appropriate mode of human awareness. The habitual egocentric mode in which man identifies himself with a subject facing a world of alien objects does not fit the physical situation."[17] Awareness of and respect for the physical situation–which Watts summarizes with the claim that "the only single event is the universe itself"–demands more than what the individual ego can offer.[18] Westerners need to cultivate a new constitution of self. By liberating the unconscious from the grips of the ego, the absolute distinctions between the self and the world vanish and a new sense of interconnection becomes manifest. This new self can only be constituted as part of nature, integrated in the cosmic scheme of life. "For here one does not face life any more; one simply is it."[19]

7

Theodore Roszak's Countercultural Challenge: Paradigm Found or Technocracy Unbound?

> Troubled by the environmental disconnection of their profession, a number of adventurous psychologists are at last seeking to create ecologically relevant forms of therapy. . . . "Ecopsychology" is the name most often used for this growing body of theory and practice, but others have been suggested: psycho-ecology, eco-therapy, global therapy, green therapy, earth-centered therapy, re-earthing. . . . The neologisms are no more euphonious than the term "psychoanalysis" was when first proposed, but by whatever name, the goal is the same: to expand the framework of psychiatric thought to include the natural environment.[1]

No scholar has articulated more concisely or completely the philosophy behind the 1960s revolution than Theodore Roszak. A professor of history and general studies, Roszak consistently delineates countercultural sensiblities in psychological terms: the reason-as-virtue consciousness which Western technocracy has so forcibly indoctrinated is being transformed by an integration of the ecological unconscious. Although he first uses the term in his latest book, *The Voice of the Earth,* the ecological unconscious is the focal point of all his work. In his groundbreaking classic, *The Making of a Counter Culture,* he not only exposes technocracy as the major culprit behind the West's stymied spiritual development, but also describes the youth's revolt as a psychic attempt to reach beyond ego consciousness. Through drugs and mysticism, the counterculture "assaults the reality of the ego as an isolable, purely cerebral unit of identity."[2] Although many of the youth's attempts at expanding consciousness were marred with perversions, the attack of the seemingly insurmountable enemy, technocracy, demanded extreme measures.

The self-sustaining power structure of technocracy, an accepted cultural imperative, enforces the dominant scientific worldview and subtly promotes the idealized illusion called the American way of life. Based on reason, knowledge, self-confidence, and objectivity, its goals are organization, efficiency, modernization, progress, leisure, comfort, and, most importantly, control. The results of its success are the death of mystery and magic, the dehumanization of its citizen-pawns, the raping of the earth, and potentially complete genocide. Despite the fact that technocracy is invisibly manipulative, its operating principle is clear: "Those who govern justify themselves by appeal to technical experts who, in turn, justify themselves by appeal to scientific forms of knowledge. And beyond the authority of science, there is no appeal."[3] This single-vision method of governance has endangered life and thrust the West into a post-Christian era without any viable connections to the ecstatic, spiritual realm. This has been done, according to Roszak, by virture of technocracy's tendency to consign nonscientific forms of knowledge to a realm of meaninglessness.

Technocracy's aggressive secular skepticism is what the counterculture wishes to reject. In its place, it attempts "to proclaim a new heaven and new earth so vast, so marvelous that the inordinate claims of technical expertise must of necessity withdraw in the presence of such splendor to a subordinate and marginal status in the lives of men." This beatific vision, the backbone of beat and hippie aesthetics, integrates ideas from the student New Left, the psychedelic drug experience, and rock-and-roll "prophets" to the Earth wisdom of ancient Eastern religions:

> The strange younsters who don cowbells and primitive talismans and who take communal ceremonies are in reality seeking to ground democracy safely beyond the culture of expertise. They give us back the image of the paleolithic band, where the community during its rituals stood in the presence of the sacred in a rude equality that predated class, state, status. It is a strange brand of radicalism we have here that turns to prehistoric precedent for its inspiration.[4]

While propagating, however crudely, Earth wisdom, the youth were demanding a reinstitution of the transrational powers repressed by over two millenia of Judeo-Christian "soul shaping" and three hundred years of intellect-oriented experts and authorities. As such, the counterculture's project equals the psychic task of resurrecting the mystical, unconscious, intuitional elements of the self. If successful, this project could initiate an "epochal transformation"—one which could balance fact and value, man and woman, civilization and nature.

As Roszak observes in *Person/Planet*, countercultural sensibilities have led Westerners to "search for a new image of nature and human identity by which to guide our lives." Not only reflected in the 1970s New Age and the human-potential and personal-growth therapies, these countercultural sensibilities have entered and pervade the daily experience of innumerable people. At home, school, work, and "in all their transactions with official authority and corporate power," people are becoming dissatisfied with "some pre-existing social slot which simply will not adapt to their shape" and are recognizing their right to create personal and spiritual authenticity. In other words, "the environmental anguish of the Earth has entered our lives as a radical transformation of human identity. The needs of the planet and the needs of the person have become one, and together they have begun to act upon the central institutions of our society with a force that is profoundly subversive, but which carries within it the promise of cultural renewal."[5]

The success of this renewal rests in the recognition of "the ecological emergency of our time for the profound spiritual failure it is." By closing the mind to "the facts of our feelings, the reality of our intuitive powers," the West has lost touch with Mother Earth and become deaf to her voice. The denunciation of "the sacred within us" began with the devaluation of the Mother Goddess symbol, which has been demoted to an aspect of the defunct Old Religion simply because its transrational meaning is empirically untenable. However, as Roszak indicates, this desensitization is being rectified. As signs of the times, the rise of feminist spirituality has become "a significant contemporary attempt to invent a new (or perhaps I should say to revive a very old) relationship to the Earth, one which grants the planet its personhood and its sacred rights"; and ecology has become a legitimate scientific enterprise as well as a means of spreading countercultural awareness.[6] While both feminist and ecological spirituality offer forms of revival of the Mother Goddess, as ideologies they are merely two in a mosaic that reflect the emergence of a new paradigm.

In *The Voice of the Earth*, Roszak describes the new paradigm in terms of a fusion of psychology, comsology, and ecology—or, more specifically, in terms of ecopsychology. His aim is to explain the following: how the reshaping of psychoanalysis (which he regards as moving from the couch to the home to the city to the biosphere) has created a larger view of the self; how the new cosmology's assimilation of the metaphysical implications of concepts such as the Anthropic and Gaian principles has led to the discovery of the self-organizing impulse—or, the evolving source of wisdom—in nature; and how ecology's understanding of nature's interconnectedness promotes a reverence for life which, in turn, reveals to its listeners the voice of the earth.

The reshaping of psychoanalysis, which he follows from Freud's reality principle to Jung's collective unconscious to Maslow's autonomous self to the ecological unconscious, denotes for Roszak a reconstitution of the context of sanity and explains how and why psychiatry is called to a revolutionary task. This task involves the creation of the awareness that "the Earth's cry for rescue from the punishing weight of the industrial system we have created is our own cry for a scale and quality of life that will free each of us to become the complete person we were born to be."[7] To create such an awareness, psychiatry would have to expand its aims and methods. Its practioners would have to stop attempting to make it merely an empirical science and accept the fact that subjectivity, participation, and feeling are necessary components in the creation of a holistic view of the self. Ever since Freud the goal has been to legitimize psychoanalysis as an enterprise of medical science, as a means to fix what is broken. Even Abraham Maslow, whose notion of self-actualization transcended Freud's medical model of the psyche, surrendered his theory to the hard sciences by failing to supply it with an ecological dimension. In other words, "what is broken" is the context in which psychiatry defines sanity–or, what is "crazy" is that psychology has limited the self to the reality principle, a principle that refuses to pay respect to the environment, that fails to put into practice the sacredness of the interconnection between humankind and nature.

Cosmology, which includes metaphysics in its purview, confirms the ecopsychological message: people are physically and spiritually linked to the cosmos. Expanding upon the recognition in the new physics that mind cannot be separated from descriptions of the forces governing nature, cosmologists have integrated concepts such as the Anthropic and Gaian principles to describe these forces. The Anthropic principle supplies cosmology with a postphysical view of matter which assimilates attributes of mind and life. Along with the concept of Gaia, which stipulates that the biosphere and all of its living ecosystems are connected in thought, the Anthropic principle offers the new cosmology an organically connected moral dimension which has been sorely lacking in the purely scientific worldview. In place of Newtonian notions such as a divine clockmaker and the great chain of being, the new cosmology explicates the roles that phenomena such as chance, randomness, coincidence, spontaneity, participation, and complementarity assume in the revelation of the sacred, animistic nature of life:

> The New Cosmology and our deepening study of ordered complexity provide the raw intellectual material for a new understanding of human connectedness with nature. In time . . . [w]e will find ourselves once again on speaking terms with nature. Within this greater environmental context, sanity and madness take on new meanings. We begin to see how the urban-industrial reality principle represses much that is essential to the health both of person and planet: the primitive, the organic, the feminine, the child-like, the wild.[8]

Ecology, the study of the interrelatedness of all things, not only coalesces with the new cosmological worldview, it has spawned movements–such as deep ecology and ecofeminism–which have inculcated concepts such as Gaia, the Mother Goddess impulse, and mind-in-nature. Hand in hand with the new cosmology, ecological awareness has challenged psychology with the following goals: to reunite the body with the self, to expand the ego beyond the realm of the reality principle, and to accept the wisdom of the id. Because ecological awareness expands the psyche by re-identifying it with the eco-aspects of the id and the unconscious, ecopsychology produces a new picture of the self, a self connected with the environment:

> Just as it has been the goal of previous therapies to recover the repressed contents of the unconscious, so the goal of ecopsychology is to awaken the inherent sense of environmental reciprocity that lies within the ecological unconscious. Other therapies seek to heal the alienation between person and person, person and family, person and society. Ecopsychology seeks to heal the more fundamental alienation between the person and the natural environment.[9]

In expounding an ecopsychology, Roszak maintains that Jung's collective unconscious is the most relevant concept inherited from mainstream modern psychology and that the id is the entity which needs the most reconsideration. The two concepts are intricately linked in Freudian theory. Freud limited the notion of a collective unconscious or collective mind to a communication of notions such as the primal horde and the murdering impulse of sons, or, to the realm of a sexually oriented id. While Roszak regards Freud's theory as too mechanistic, too willing to sacrifice the spirit to the body, he sees Jung's as being too much like Plato's Forms, too willing to sacrifice the body to the spirit. An immense reservoir of humankind's great religious archetypes and symbols, Jung's collective unconscious became more and more spiritual and cultural and less and less like the primitive instincts of humankind's physical evolution. While Freud's theory fails miserably in an ecopsychological framework, Jung's at least has potential—particularly when linked to a refined, more holistic understanding of the id.

The id, according to Roszak, is "the protohuman psychic core that our environment has spent millions of years molding to fit the planetary environment."[10] By regarding the id as an infantile aspect of the psyche which is properly controlled and directed by the adult ego and the corresponding reality principle, Freud and subsequent psychoanalysts have de-sanctified it, adding but another dimension to Western civilization's "war with nature." Only by reconsidering the significance of the id can the traditionally regarded atomistic ego be transformed into an ecological ego, an ego that speaks for rather than against the ecological unconscious. In other words, the interrelationship between the id and ecological unconscious inevitably binds the psyche to the universe. At its most profound level, Roszak explains, the collective unconscious

> shelters the compacted ecological intelligence of our species, the source from which culture finally unfolds as the self-conscious reflection of nature's own steadily emergent mindlikeness. . . . It was there to guide that development by trial and error, selection and extinction, as it was there in the instant of the Big Bang to congeal the first flash of radiation into the rudiments of durable matter. It is *this* id with which the ego must unite if we are to become a sane species capable of greater evolutionary adventures.[11]

A return to the evolutionary-ecological sources of the id would transform the context of sanity by including the biosphere. To encourage such a transformation, ecopsychology turns to many sources, such as the Mother Goddess impulse and the traditional healing techniques of primal peoples, and applies them to the goal of creating an ecological ego. In so doing, ecopsychology offers people the opportunity to revitalize in contemporary culture traces of the ancient wisdom which unites the self and cosmos. This unity, which Roszak regards as the ultimate goal of the new paradigm, was the revolutionary aim—however brash and narcissistic their experiments were—of the 1960s youth. To experience the animism declared as sacred by primary people was inherent in all the various attempts at self-actualization correlative to emergent countercultural sensibilities. Although the counterculture "has become less visible over the past decade[s] only because it has dissolved into its surrounding social medium," through its connection to movements such as deep ecology, ecofeminism, and the Greens, it continues to promote the shift to the new paradigm.[12]

8

Fritjof Capra's Call for a Coup d'Tao

> I believe that the world view implied by modern physics is inconsistent with our present society, which does not reflect the harmonious interrelatedness we observe in nature. To achieve such a state of dynamic balance, a radically different social and economic structure will be needed: a cultural revolution in the true sense of the word. The survival of our whole civilization may depend on whether we can bring about such a change. It will depend, ultimately, on our ability to adopt some of the yin attitudes of Eastern mysticism: to experience the wholeness of nature and the art of living with it in harmony.[1]

Fritjof Capra's holistic, synthetic approach used in creating his highly popular version of the new paradigm epitomizes the way in which the tradition's enormous scopes and complex perspectives can be fused so specifically with the one concrete mandate to revere the balance of nature's polarities. Using his own research in high-energy physics and the theories of philosophers, mythologists, sociologists, anthropologists, biologists, ecologists, and feminists, Capra supplies the scientific worldview emerging from the findings of the new physics with a spiritual dimension; outlines the needed changes for and the potential ramifications of a successful cultural transformation in terms of psychology, religion, politics, science, economics, and health; and calls for the coalescence of all countercultural ideologies under the banner of the Green movement.

While investigating in *The Tao of Physics* the similar ways in which Eastern mystics and quantum theorists describe the universe, Capra begins his assault on the patriarchal worldview. His major point of attack is the West's perception of the cosmos as a mechanical system composed of elementary building blocks. This perception started with Democritus and the logical atomists of ancient Greece; culminated in Descartes' and Newton's cause-and-effect description of a universe divinely governed by rationally ascertainable natural laws; and ended with the spiritless, totally mechanical understanding of the universe. The Newtonian worldview, despite its recent collapse via the emergence of a new scientific paradigm, still holds the imagination of society at large. This view is the product of science's relentless aim to explain the whole in terms of its component parts. The new physics, Capra argues, recognizes that processes underlie all structures and that these processes necessarily assimilate such concepts as chance, chaos, participation, complementarity, and relativity into the new worldview—a view which is surprisingly consistent with the multimillenarian wisdom of Eastern mystics.

Eastern mystics have always recognized the relativity of space and time as well as the preeminence of intuition over reason and the whole over its parts. At the very core of Buddhist, Hindu, and Taoist philosophy resides an awareness that all phenomena interpenetrate, that things and events are manifestations of one reality. This awareness, Capra insists, is slowly finding its way into the worldview of contemporary Western science. For instance, quantum theorists unexpectedly began finding that the deeper they delved into the nature of subatomic existence, the more this existence revealed its interconnectedness. They also gradually realized that there is no way of observing what is subatomically happening without influencing what is happening. For example, when a photon is "asked a question" about its wave-like quality, it will answer as a wave; yet when it is asked about its particle quality, it will answer as a particle. In the same way, the dynamic network of subatomic nature as a whole cannot be broken down in any meaningful sense. It is so intricately interdependent that investigative results can only be documented in terms of probabilities and tendencies. Unlike Newtonian or classical mechanics, modern physics shows that matter can no longer be considered an accumulation of isolated, microscopic objects or particles; rather, the universe itself is an entity in which each particle contains all particles. In other words, the cosmos is a field-connected substance united by interpenetrating processes.

Physicists have recognized also that our concepts of space and time are practical yet superficial projections that the mind uses to help fit things and events into successions of cause and effect. Modern physics has revolutionized the classical notion that space and time are separate, absolute dimensions which exist independent of the material world. Space and time are not only relative to the observer, in Capra's words, "they are unified into a four-dimensional continuum in which the particle interactions can stretch in any direction."[2] Hence, any attempt to measure space and time or particles and structures in absolute terms loses all significance.

The inability to dissect, analyze, and explain reality is particularly evident, Capra maintains, in the descriptive limitations of ordinary language, limitations which mystics have always recognized and which the new physicists have—with great difficulty—realized only recently. The poetry of the *Tao Te Ching*, the mythology of *The Bhagavad Gita*, and the transrational nature of Zen koans all point to a reality which is intuitively, not analytically, comprehensible. The new physicists were forced into this realm simply because the reality that they were discovering could not be described in mechanical terms. As Einstein admits, it was as if the ground on which scientists stood had been pulled out from under them by the quantum and relativity theories and there was no scientific language cabable of describing what nature was expressing.[3]

The participatory nature of the universe forces the realization that truth is not "out there" to be objectively verified; rather, it is our inner relationship with or the intuitive experience of the outside world which captures the interconnectedness of cosmic processes. As such, the findings of Western science and Eastern mysticism convey—Capra insists—a very similar worldview, one which accords reality an ecological, spiritual dimension. As he explains in *Belonging to the Universe*, "The worldview now emerging from modern science is an ecological view," which is why the new paradigm "is accompanied by a new rise of spirituality, particularly a new kind of earth-centered spirituality."[4]

By outlining six criteria of new-paradigm thinking in science, Capra reveals what he considers to be the spiritual dimension inherent in the new physics. Briefly, here are the criteria formulated in terms of the paradigm shift: the dynamics of the whole are now more preeminent in understanding the nature of reality than are its constituent parts; the notion of solid, atomistic structures has given way to the concept of a web of relationships in which structures are recognized as secondary to processes; the myth of an objective science has been replaced by an epistemic science which takes into account the participation of consciousness in observing and describing natural phenomena; the building-block metaphor has been supplanted by the network metaphor; the notion of absolute truth has been abandoned in favor of approximate descriptions; the attitude of domination and control of nature has been changed to one of cooperation and nonviolence. In line with these criteria, Capra asserts, "It is becoming ever more apparent that mysticism, or the perennial philosophy . . . provides the most consistent philosophical background to the new scientific paradigm."[5]

What makes the similarities between the six scientific criteria and Eastern mystics' understanding of reality so significant is the growing cultural context in which these similarities are now being articulated. According to Capra, his theme in *The Tao of Physics* has been made "much clearer by being reformulated and put in a larger conceptual context." This context stipulates that "we are embedded in the multiple alternative networks of what I have called the 'rising culture'–a multitude of movements representing different facets of the same new vision of reality, gradually coalescing to form a powerful force of social transformation."[6] The convergence of Eastern philosophy and Western science is, then, only one manifestation of a greater cultural transformation.

In *The Turning Point*, Capra expands the context of his cultural transformation theory by describing how the yin-yang theory serves as a model for understanding and solving the imbalances prevalent in the West's values and attitudes. Drawing support from the *I Ching*, *Tao Te Ching* and *Chuang Tzu*, he associates yin with responsive, cooperative, and consolidating activity and yang with competitive, aggressive, and expanding activity. While yin action is oriented toward the environment, yang action is oriented toward the self; hence, the first may be regarded as eco-action and the second as ego-action. He stresses that neither mode of activity is good or bad; rather, the balance of the two modes may be regarded as healthy and their imbalance as harmful. The fact that the West overemphasizes the masculine, yang, aggressive, and rational powers at the expense of feminine, yin, responsive, and intuitive ones can be observed on a daily basis in news reports. The West's current epidemic scales of inflation, starvation, unemployment, crime, disease, lack of health care, and pollution are all part of a crisis of perception–a crisis resulting from Westerners allowing intuitive-yin capabilities to degenerate by overestimating the powers of the yang-intellect.

To advance his theme, Capra merges his yin-yang model with the systems theory of modern science. Like the yin-yang model, "systems theory looks at the world in terms of the interrelatedness and interdependence of all phenomena, and in this framework an integrated whole whose properties cannot be reduced to those of its parts is called a system."[7]

Of his numerous examples of ways in which systems theory substantiates the yin-yang model, the most comprehensive one concerns the systems view of mind. This view delineates how all living systems–cells, the earth, the universe–possess faculties of mind with opposing yet harmonious qualities. All living systems are both parts and wholes (e.g., organelles are wholes in that they are self-regulating systems, yet they are parts of cells), and, as such, have two modes of operation. Using Arthur Koestler's concept of "holons" to describe the operation of these systems/subsystems, Capra explains that a holon possesses two opposite tendencies: an integrative one and a self-assertive one. The fact that these two tendencies are opposite but complementary can be observed in a healthy system, in which the two tendencies are balanced. "This balance is not static but consists of a dynamic interplay between the two complementary tendencies, which makes the whole system flexible and open to change."[8] Koestler's notion of holons reflects the wisdom of Taoism simply because a balance of the self-assertive yang and integrative yin tendencies is imperative for harmonious social and ecological relationships.

These tendencies are manifest in two opposing views of nature, as a source of goods to be dominated and manipulated (a yang perspective) and as a living organism to be revered and nurtured (a yin perspective). The first view is epitomized by the

Newtonian-Cartesian paradigm, which regards cells, humans, and the earth as isolated entities which operate in rationally understandable ways, as does a well-made clock. The second view, which Capra supports with J. E. Lovelock's concept of Gaia, regards the universe as a living being which breathes, thinks, and operates cyclically. This understanding, though supported by science, transcends science because of its spiritual dimensions.

Another example of Capra's use of the systems theory to reaffirm the yin-yang model is his contention that a systems view of mind renders perspectives of the psyche that extend beyond the traditional psychological approach. As a bio-psychological entree, he points to the dual-brain theory (popularized in the seventies by Robert Ornstein) which, based on the research of split-brain patients, states that the brain's right hemisphere specializes in holistic, synthetic, transrational functions and the left hemisphere in linear, analytic, rational ones. The deep-rooted preference for the left brain, which characterizes Western societies, is related to centuries of domination by the patriarchal value system.

As examples of psychological attempts to create a view of a balanced psyche, Capra injects brief analyses of the psychological theories of William James, Carl Jung, and Ken Wilber. James was the first psycholgist to fervently criticize the mechanistic tendencies in psychology and to advocate the interconnectedness of mind and body. Similarly, adds Capra, Jung worked to extend the inquiries of psychology beyond the realm of a mechanical science. Jung's understanding of the psyche as a self-regulating dynamic system, characterized by fluctuations between opposite poles, helped psychoanalysis to transcend Freud's mechanistic model of the id, ego, and super-ego. For these reasons, James and Jung can be regarded rightfully as revolutionary new-paradigm psychologists.

Capra regards Ken Wilber's spectrum psychology as one of the most comprehensive syntheses of different psychological schools. While unifying both Eastern and Western approaches, Wilber has created a view of human consciousness which ranges from the confined ego to cosmic consciousness. Of the four basic levels he distinguishes between in *The Spectrum of*

Consciousness, Wilber puts the transpersonal level at the apex of his psychological hierarchy–a level which Capra equates with Jung's collective unconscious.[9] In short, Capra sees in Wilber's theory, as in James's and Jung's, a delineation of yin and yang qualities which holistically depict a balanced psyche.

In Capra's scheme, then, the systems approach designates not only a reshaping of physics but of psychology as well. As he argues in *Uncommon Wisdom,* this reshaping is evident in the fact "that many of the differences between Freud and Jung parallel those between classical and modern physics." Claiming that Freud clung to the Cartesian paradigm by refusing to orient his theories beyond the scope of the psyche as a conglomeration of specific mechanisms, Capra avers that Jung, with his notion of the collective unconscious, based many of his theories on the connections among the individual, the human species, and the biosphere as a whole, connections "which cannot be understood within a mechanistic framework." Because Jung regarded the unconscious as dynamic patterns of relationships "in which each archetype, ultimately, involves all the others," his notion of "psychic energy," though imbued with a scientifically quantitative flavor, can be easily correlated with the concept of energy emerging from the new physics.[10] In Capra's words:

> Once I had put the systems view of life in the center of my synthesis of the new paradigm, it became relatively easy to see that Jung's theory of psychic energy could be reformulated in modern systems language and thus made consistent with the most advanced current developments in the life sciences.[11]

What the new-paradigm shift in science and psychology has meant in terms of a new worldview, ecology and feminism have meant for Western culture as a whole. Both movements, Capra insists, not only stemmed from the sixties consciousness but also provided a framework for developing and critiquing the alternative ideas and values that were embodied by the hippies in the sixties and were articulated by new-paradigm scholars in the seventies. The spirituality which fuses the two movements centers on the feminine principle, Mother Earth. As such, ecology and feminism equal two unique manifestations of the same impulse.

This spirituality was embraced politically by the world-wide Green movement which emerged from a coalescence of the peace, femininist, and ecology movements. The success of the Greens–which he considers to be "the most impressive sign of the political activity of the eighties"–was achieved (particularly in Germany) by their self-acclaimed non-party platform, which included a significant number of women in important positions, was characterized by casual dress and appearance, and involved clear and direct statements regarding issues.[12] In *Green Politics*, Capra and co-author Charlene Spretnak maintain that the Greens' unwritten manifesto

> emphasizes the interconnectedness and interdependence of all phenomena, as well as the embeddedness of individuals and societies in the cyclical processes of nature. It addresses the unjust and destructive dynamics of patriarchy. It calls for social responsibility and a sound, sustainable economic system, one that is ecological, decentralized, equitable, and comprised of flexible institutions, one in which people have significant control over their lives. In advocating a cooperative world order, Green politics rejects all forms of exploitation–of nature, individuals, social groups, and countries. It is committed to nonviolence at all levels. It encourages a rich cultural life that respects the pluralism within a society, and it honors the inner growth that leads to wisdom and compassion. Green politics, in short, is the political manifestation of the cultural shift to the new paradigm.[13]

What Green politics represents for Capra, then, is the social interaction of the new value system with the new views of self and cosmos emerging from the fields of psychology and physics, respectively. Capra claims that he would like to call the movement behind the new-paradigm shift the Green movement, but because of the inability of the deep ecologists, ecofeminists, psychotherapists, and countercultural ideologists as a whole to unite under the banner of the Greens, the force behind the cultural transformation remains a rather disassembled one.

In sum, Capra's version of the new paradigm is psychologically and scientifically grounded in systems theory, a theory supremely expressed in the model of the harmonious interaction between yin and yang. This model, as delineated in Capra's scheme, provides an alternative worldview and value system aimed at circumventing the life-threatening spiritual crisis of Western civilization. Essential to the impending cultural transformation is a shift away from the view of the body, psyche, and universe as separate mechanical systems toward one of physical and spiritual interconnectedness.

9

Sam Keen's Erotic Ideal: From Androgyne to Lover

> As it becomes increasingly clear in the next decades that we have to choose between human survival and the warfare system, between a green earth and ever-expanding populations and industrial economies, the Spirit that moves within history to bring hope out of despair and life out of death will invite us into a new American revolution. You may be certain the decade ahead will be interesting and chaotic.[1]

With the exception of his first book (*Apology for Wonder*), Sam Keen's version of the new-paradigm message relies more on his own experience than on the research of other scholars' theories, more on his own story-telling ability than on the edification of a logical argument. In his uninhibited, colloquial style he describes his own heroic journey with sparse allusions to interpretations of mainstream psychology's archetypal hero's journey. Whether describing his sexual or drug experiences or manifestations of his psychological crisis, Keen openly confronts the pathologies associated with the different levels and processes of self-transformation, processes which equal the assimilation of the new paradigm into a contemporary life-style. Always ready to offer advice, Keen sees his work as allowing his readers "to take the spiritual drama of their own lives seriously": "My decision to trust my experience more than any dogma, church, guru, or authority encouraged others to do the same and began a movement that brought the notion of story-telling back into the center of theology where it belongs."[2]

In *Apology for Wonder* Keen utilizes the Nietzschean distinction between the Apollonian and Dionysian impulses to key his own new-paradigm scheme. He begins by dividing humankind into four descriptive (not generic) types: homo admirans (wondering "man"); homo faber (technological man); homo ludens (playing man); and homo tempestivus (ecological man). His category of traditional wondering man includes primal, ancient Greek, and early Christian man—or those who sustained the sanctity of life through wonder.

> Primal man knew little of the hard-and-fast distinctions that Western thought has come to make between the animate and the inanimate, the natural and the supernatural, the material and the mental, the secular and the religious, or the factual and the symbolic. The chief rule of life was continuity rather than discontinuity; men, stars, animals, and gods were all related in a family way: all things were bound together in the economy of the cosmos.[3]

Although Keen sees a continuity between primal and Greek thought, the first step in the creation of the modern technological man occurred with the shift from primal man's contemplative wonder to ancient Greek philosophers' (particularly Plato's) theoretical wonder. This shift helped supplant the Mother Earth religion of primal man with the philosophy of logos, the truth of mythology with the truth of rational knowledge. With the advent of the Christian logos, Keen claims that the immanent divine mind as developed by the Greeks became transcendent. This shift, by de-sanctifying the earth and the body, broke the continuity achieved by primal and Greek man and paved the way for the emergence of homo faber, a twentieth-century creature whose Apollonian drive has brought about "the death of God, the loss of the holy, the secularization of Western culture, and the loss of cosmic reason."[4]

This does not mean that Christianity originated as an Apollonian religion. On the contrary, Keen insists that "Christianity emerged as the advocate of Dionysus." Jesus' teachings declared that "love is ontologically more fundamental than law, and therefore the authentic man is free from cosmic and moral legalism." A rebellion against the repressive powers of Roman and Hebraic patriarchy, early Christianity embraced "the divine power that grants ecstasy, freedom, and novelty." However, the life and teachings of Jesus became the word or logos, a concept which Church fathers and Christian culture gradually refined in the process of rejecting Christianity's Dionysian origins. By developing their own version of Apollonian legalism and orthodoxy, Christian dogmatists stressed that "Christ was the definitive intrusion of the divine into history," a position which necessitated the Christian community's shift of emphasis on the sacred dimension of here and now (the Kingdom within) to the "remembrance of things past and hope for things to come" (the Kingdom in heaven).[5] By separating the sacred from the profane, Christian doctrine demonized the body, the id, ecstasy, and nature.

The separation of the sacred spiritual realm from the profane physical realm, in turn, allowed the blades of science to chop the spirit cleanly away from human life. By making logos a cold, scientific principle, technological man has infused his chaotic, chance-oriented worldview with a pathological frenzy of nothingness, absurdity, and pluralism. Wrapped in the conviction that common sense and convention provide the only viable means of determining individual identity and of governing social interaction, homo faber crowned himself lord over nature.

According to Keen, the obsessive implementation of this conviction has led, inevitably, to a contemporary "Dionysian revolution." The revolution has put into question the entire moral fabric of homo faber and opened the horizon to a multitude of potential types of man—the most prominent being homo ludens and homo tempestivus. While leisure time and hedonistic pursuits characterize homo ludens, homo tempestivus (or "the man for all seasons") represents the authentic, healthy human who has learned to balance Apollo with Dionysus. Like primal man, homo tempestivus trusts nature; but like modern man, he has confidence in his ability "to undertake appropriate action." In other words, he is the model human who "avoids the extremes that lead to the Apollonian and Dionysian pathologies without sacrificing the virtues of either god."[6]

In *Life Maps* (co-authored with Jim Fowler), Keen again uses Nietzsche's model, but this time to delineate his Dionysian approach to psychoanalysis and to address the West's imbalance in terms of male and female virtues. With very little recourse to Greek myth and a great deal of his own psychoanalytic vernacular, he argues that Dionysus represents the personality's passional and disordering principles while the Apollonian "is the glue that keeps the ego together." Unlike his "Apollonian colleague" (Fowler), he claims that he does not stress the similarity between faith and the ordering principle; rather, he emphasizes the relationship of trust to the emotional and the dynamic processes of the constantly changing personality. Keen sees the Dionysian impulse as a way to escape boundaries set by the ego–to open to a force existing at the very heart of nature. He is convinced that by breaking down the personality and destroying character, the human being creates a center outside of the self: "In Nietzsche's terms, trust is the confidence that the center is everywhere. I focus on the pluralism that allows personality to disintegrate in a creative way, on the divine madness that allows us to lose ourselves." By submitting to the passionate, disordering principles, people allow themselves to be "moved by a power beyond."[7] To Keen, trust in nature's power is the essence of the Dionysian impulse. By obeying the body as well as the mind, one relinquishes some of the control which renders one separate from others as well as from nature.

Depicting Apollonian forces as male-oriented and the Dionysian as female-oriented, Keen argues that in the West

> the highest value is assigned to mind, head, reason, control, rationality, technique–that is, to what traditionally have been the 'masculine' virtues. The 'feminine' virtues, which are associated with body knowledge, touch, emotion, surrender, and art, are less highly valued. Control is up. Being controlled is down. . . . In a capitalized society, mind governs matter, capital governs labor, the head governs the body.[8]

What society needs to create, Keen insists, is the awareness that in order to control the destructive urges one must stay in touch with them. To cast a veil over the darker impulses is neither practical nor healthy, simply because Apollo and Dionysus belong together.

The reason that the Apollonian consciousness rebukes the Dionysian experience is because it "breaks into and destroys the human categories of understanding, shattering the nice coherences we have managed to make. It fractures the intellect." This, in turn, explains why Apollonians are terrified of the thought of losing control, let alone madness. "Their fear is that if we had emotional freedom, it would lead to uncorseted excess. This is not true . . . . We need both fierceness and tenderness, both discipline and love, both moderation and excess."[9] To recognize the harmony in the impulses' discord is, as Keen concludes in *Life Maps*, to recognize that all humans are "androgynous" beings and that what is lacking in Western society is the proper integration of masculine and feminine virtues.

> There is a paradox in being androgynous, in realizing our capacity for love and evil, for male and female, for Apollo and Dionysus. If we see our capacity to be cruel, we may also begin to understand our ability to be loving and nurturing.[10]

In *The Passionate Life: Stages of Loving*, Keen constructs a "life-map," or "an outline of an erotic developmental psychology," which "traces the transformations of love throughout an *ideal* lifetime."[11] The five levels of this development (which he outlines in *Life Maps* and develops in *The Passionate Life*) are the Child, Rebel, Adult, Outlaw, and Lover/Fool. By delineating these stages of transformation, Keen hopes to reveal that, "in capsule form, the history of the decline and fall of love can be traced in the changed meaning of the word 'erotic.'" As he appropriately suggests, Greek philosophers regarded eros as "the prime mover, the motivating principle in all things human and nonhuman. It was the impulse that made all things yearn and strive for fulfillment." While an acorn is "erotically moved" to become an oak tree, a human is moved by the power of eros toward self-actualization–a principle inherent to Dionysianism. However, Western civilization has limited eros to a sexual meaning, thus instigating and maintaining "our alienation from the rest of nature."[12] Besides exposing the pathologies associated with "being stuck" in each of the first four stages, Keen describes the final erotic transformation of the Outlaw (or androgynous psyche) to the Lover (or balanced self).

The first two stages, the Child and Rebel, represent the oral and anal stages of Freudian psychology and, as such, need to be transcended before one reaches adulthood. The perversion of eros begins with the social conditioning power of norms, or the rules which are aimed at the child's erotic deprivation. Being completely dependent, the child quickly accepts that, for instance, touching the "wrong" place or person at the "wrong" time for the "wrong" reasons are taboos which are naturally accompanied by guilt and shame; that passion is governed by a system of "oughts" which directs the release of passion toward "our class, our clan, our look alikes"; and that being good is a matter of conforming to the voices of authority.[13] To be arrested in this stage of development means that one has not succeeded in separating oneself from the matrix, the comforting womb and the providing Mother, and, hence, remains a creature of dependence with only a shell of identity.

While the child is, in Keen's terms, wounded by the conventions, the erotic desensitizations, and the repressive super-ego cultivated by civilization, the rebel gladly and angrily revolts against all that society has imposed as norms. The rebel's ability to say "no," to create his or her own values, helps him or her to establish self-identity. By severing the bonds of childhood, the rebel begins the process of individuation, a process which–when the rebellion is properly accepted–helps build to a resonant adult life. However, the danger of rebellion is that it may become embedded in one's character armor and, hence, will never be fully accepted or overcome. Perversely, eros has gone awry, for the goal of fulfillment is substituted by obsessions of possessiveness and resentment. A rebel who has not learned to "rebond" himself or herself with others is easily engulfed by paranoia and consequently becomes an adversary of the self by remaining an adversary of others.

The adult has successfully established his or her character and, freely or not so freely, affirmed the values of culture. This individual has become a citizen committed to the goals of society, initiated through the rites of passage and fully integrated with the social body. In line with the socially cherished notion of normality, women learn tenderness and domesticity and men learn to be fierce warriors. The accepted role divisions form a "consensual schizophrenia" which, according to Keen, reveals the perversity of using normality as a yardstick of sanity. To be an adult, the man is expected to dominate and the woman is expected to submit, expectations which become huge enemies of eros. Instead of aiming at self-fulfillment, the adult aims at becoming half a person, an ego without an unconscious, a man without feminine traits or a female without masculine traits. This battle-oriented mentality, Keen declares, resides at the very origins of Western civilization.

The way out of society's erotic-repressing dualism is to adopt the outlaw's breach with normality, embrace of nature, and "quest for androgyny." Free of all character armor, the outlaw accepts the erotic goal of transformation and looks beyond the duties and roles of being an adult to find a world which is filled with mystery, ecstasy, and madness–the world of eros. Although the outlaw is cast into the realm beyond good and evil, of eternal doubt, of the terror of the void, the outlaw has overcome the stereotypes associated with normality and, in so doing, has reaffirmed his or her place in nature-beyond-culture. "To reclaim the full range of the eros of the self," Keen insists, "I must heal the schizophrenia that exists within myself between my 'masculine' (approved and socially reinforced, since I am a male) and my 'feminine' side (disowned, repressed, and therefore largely unconscious)."[14] Despite the value of recognizing one's androgynous nature, it is not the final stage in the transformation of eros, simply because the fulfillment achieved is strictly noncommunal. To remain stuck in this stage leads one to confuse self-love with narcissism, self-knowledge with solipsism, power with self-assertiveness, and virtue with amorality.

To achieve a true erotic self, one must assimilate the self-actualization achieved by the outlaw with the full potential of the other–friends, society, and the environment. In other words, the lover has learned to balance the outlaw's sense of self with the cosmos: "Our erotic potential is fulfilled only when we become cosmopolitan lovers, only when *potentia* (power) and *eros* (desire) reunite our bodies to the *polis* (the body politic) and the *cosmos* (the natural environment)."[15] For a lover who has experienced the community of the biosphere, ecological awareness becomes a passion, a passion which, when enacted, becomes compassion:

> Our relationship to our bodies, to our land, to our sexuality is singular, cut from the same model. We cohabit either lovingly or carelessly.

> And our erotic impulses are fully satisfied only when we are within an environment in which we are continually stimulated to care and to enjoy. Eros is fully engaged only when we make the cosmic connection.[16]

The travels through the five stages of the ideal passionate life, Keen insists, equal a truly heroic journey. Throughout his work, he avers his particular place at a particular time in this journey. In *Life Maps*, he is reluctant to even describe the realm of the lover because he regards himself as more of an outlaw; in *The Passionate Life* he reveals himself as gradually transforming into a lover; and in *Fire in the Belly: On Being a Man* he defines, theoretically and experientially, what it is to be a lover. By re-assessing the goals of the male's heroic journey, reconstituting his rites of passage, and refocusing the qualities of masculinity, *Fire in the Belly* redefines what it means to be a man. It exemplifies the final stage of the transformation of eros in masculine terms, and exposes the facts that "men cannot find themselves without first separating from the world of WOMAN"; that "our [men's] modern rites of passage–war, work, and sex–impoverish and alienate men"; and that "authentic manhood has always been defined by a vision of how we fit into the universe and by the willingess to undertake an appropriate task or vocation–which have changed at various times in history."[17] The aim of the book is to sketch the new spiritual journey men of our time must make to become whole, the heroic virtues the new man must acquire, and the manner in which the new man reconciles himself with woman.

According to Keen, ever since the notion of God as a woman, Mother Earth, became "God the Father," the symbols and goals of the mythology and the rites of passage concerning men have represented obsessively the separation of man from woman–who represents nature's creative matrix and erotic-spiritual power. While the separation is necessary for man to recognize his full identity as a polar, yet complementary force of nature, the absolute manner in which Western civilization has portrayed and encouraged the separation is nothing short of pathological. This split is personified through man's self-acclaimed roles as provider, protector, controller, and punisher, as well as his obsession with aggressiveness, insensitivity, and rationality. Consequently, "the 'war between the sexes' is no joke . . ."

> but the psychological reality that goes on constantly just beneath the masks of civility we have conspired to wear to satisfy our mutual needs. But the divorce statistics, the scarcity of joyful marriages, the frequency of rape are grim testimonies to the sexual wounds that accompany the 'normal' rites that initiate us into the role our society expects men and women to play. To be a contemporary man, or a woman, is to have a fault-line running down the center of our being, and to be less than half a person.[18]

The new heroic man and the correlative rites of passage heal the wounds between man and woman by reconstituting the feminine side of masculinity. As such, "the new heroic man is nearly the opposite of the traditional hero."[19] He has regained the powers of wonder, sensitivity, and empathy as well as the virtues of communion, husbandry, and eroticism. The new man is as fierce as the old, but now the fierceness is displayed through his compassion and moral outrage. The new man is the true lover of himself, his mate, and the cosmos.

In sum, Keen's work, culminating in *Fire in the Belly*, presents a new heroic myth which erotically unites the self and cosmos and erotically affirms the new paradigm in contemporary life. A sign of the times, the new balance between humanity's archetypal relationship to the matrix and "patrix" of the universe is reaching a climax:

> Alongside the dominant culture, an alternative culture is emerging. Feminism, the ecological movement, the new physics, the antiwar movement, appropriate technology, humanistic psychology, are the tip of the iceberg of the new myth that grows stronger as the energy crisis and the arms race bring us to the consciousness that we are at an end of the old paradigm. We stand at the edge of understanding the myths, the roles, the political forms that have in-formed our psyches.[20]

10

Riane Eisler's Archaeological Interpretation: A Gylanic Mandate

> [The] fundamental paradigm shift in archeological and religious history is directly relevant to our mounting social and ecological crises. For ours is a time when one more war could be our last, a time when both women and men are reexamining conventional assumptions about such basic issues as what is "masculine" and "feminine," and the relationship between the two. It is a time of rapid social change when we are searching for viable alternatives for our future—alternatives that findings from archeological and religious studies now indicate may, in fact, be deeply rooted in millenia-long traditions we are currently reclaiming from our past.[1]

Like Rachel Carson (*Silent Spring*), Carolyn Merchant (*The Death of Nature*), and Rosemary Radford Ruether (*New Woman/New Earth*), Riane Eisler has helped synthesize ecofeminist sensibilities. A peace activist who studied law, Eisler made popular in *The Chalice and the Blade: Our History, Our Future* both the ecofeminist-related findings of modern archaeology and the term "cultural transformation theory." The book represents "a cooperative effort" (e.g., Marija Gimbutas, Merlin Stone, and Fritjof Capra "made important contributions") as well as Eisler's personal "life-long quest"—namely, to understand why humans chronically lean "toward cruelty rather than kindness, toward war rather than peace, toward destruction rather than actualization." Building on the findings and theories of scholars such as Gimbutas (*Goddesses and Gods of Old Europe*) and Stone (*When God Was a Woman*), Eisler pieces together "our past" with an eye to securing "our future." She is concerned with a past which archaeology has started only recently to uncover. This past refers to a prehistorical, prepatriarchal time when humans lived in harmony with nature. She believes that the reverence for nature reflected in the Neolithic, gylanic social structure and spirituality not only "provides verification that a better future *is* possible," but could be adopted to support an ecofeminist ideology which could help *make* a better future.[2] Despite the fact that she continually emphasizes the need for a balance between masculine and feminine principles, she presents a feminist mandate.

The key concept in Eisler's archaeological interpretation is "gylany"—a term she juxtaposes with "androcracy." Androcracy refers to the social system imposed by patriarchal societies. The term derives from the Greek roots *andros* and *kratos*, which mean "man" and "ruled," respectively. Androcracy, she claims, refers to a system in which men rule "through force or the threat of force." Gylany, on the other hand, derives from the Greek roots "gyne," "lyein" or "lyo," and "andros." While "gy" refers to woman and "an" to man, the letter "l"—which means "to solve or resolve (as in ana*l*ysis) and to dissolve or set free (as in cata*l*ysis)" refers to "the *linking* of both halves of humanity."[3] While androcracy, then, implies a dominating model of rule, gylany reflects a partnership model of coexistence.

Her attempt to interpret archaeological data to support a cultural transformation theory which, in turn, supports the necessity of ecofeminist ideology, centers on the invasions of hunter-warrior nomads (the Kurgans/Indo-Europeans). With their patriarchal sky gods and authoritarian and hierarchic social structure, the invaders accounted for the gradual destruction of a Neolithic, matrilinial, agricultural, non-violent, Mother Goddess-worshipping way of life which existed from what is now Portugal and Crete to India and China. This theory is primarily the result of the expansive archaeological findings of Gimbutas, who argues that the Old European (which Eisler refers to as Neolithic) culture and the Kurgan culture were antithetical, the first being matrilinear and matrilocal egalitarians and the second being patrilineal, nomadic, socially stratified hunters and herders. Old European culture lived in carefully planned communities which, as attested to by their lack of weapons and fortifications, peacefully communicated, worked, and traded with one another. The Kurgans, on the other hand, "lived in small villages or seasonal settlements while grazing their animals over vast areas. One economy based on farming, the other on stock breeding and grazing, produced two contrasting ideologies." As Gimbutas concludes in "The First Wave of Eurasian Steppe Pastoralists into Copper Age Europe":

> The Old European belief system focused on the agricultural cycle of birth, death, and regeneration, embodied in the feminine principle, a Mother Creatrix. The Kurgan ideology, as known from comparitive Indo-European mythology, exalted virile, heroic warrior gods of the shining and thunderous sky. Weapons are nonexistent in Old European imagery; whereas the dagger and battle-axe are dominant symbols of the Kurgans, who like all historically known Indo-Europeans, glorified the lethal power of the sharp blade.[4]

According to Eisler, the Kurgan incursion brought about a cultural transformation with a chaos and violence that dwarfs that of any world war. Between the first and third invasions, circa 4300-4200 and 3000-2800 B.C. respectively, the Kurgans from the cold and barren North physically and spiritually subdued the rich agricultural societies that, by some 7,000 B.C., had domesticated plants and animials; learned the principles of construction, architecture, city-planning, manufacturing, and trade; practiced social equality; and, "above everything," united in the worship of nature. In so doing, the Kurgans spread the germ which ages of patriarchal civilizations cultivated and inevitably crowned in gods like Jahweh and endeavors like world wars.

Unlike the aggressive, violent, competitive, and totalitarian dominator model of these patriarchal societies, the gylanic or partnership model of the Neolithic races, Eisler submits, supplies an alternative way of life–one of peaceful coexistence. By adopting a social system which is "primarily based on the principle of *linking* rather than ranking," contemporary culture could alleviate many of the ills that have permeated the dominator model for millenia. The archaeological icons, which serve as metaphors of the respective models, are the chalice, which represents the generative and nurturing powers so highly revered in Neolithic times, and the blade, which symbolizes "technologies designed to destroy and dominate."[5] There is a lesson to be learned from the the clash of the respective social structures:

> Now, thousands of years later, when we are nearing the possibility of a second social transformation–this time a shift from a dominator society to a more advanced version of a partnership society–we need to understand everything we can about this astonishing piece of our lost past. For at stake at this second evolutionary crossroads, when we possess the technologies of total destruction once attributed only to God, may be nothing less than the survival of our species.[6]

Eisler supports her cultural transformation theory with interpretations of religious myths which tell of a time of Neolithic peace as well as a time of the patriarchal incursion. The biblical Garden of Eden relates to the former time in which women, men, and nature lived as one. The *Tao Te Ching* describes a similar period in which the yin or feminine principle was not stifled by the yang or masculine principle, "a time when the wisdom of the mother was still honored and followed above all." Hesiod also explicates a time in which a "golden race" of planters lived in "peaceful ease" before a "lesser race" disrupted this peace by introducing their god of war.[7] Eisler also uses Erich Neumann's "goddess of opposites" to stipulate how the mythological principles of femininity and masculinity as well as creation and destruction unite in the Mother Goddess impulse.

While she conveys her understanding of the myths representing gylanic societies in terms of the partnership model, a number of dominator-oriented myths–such as Apollo's slaying of the priestess-protecting serpent at Delphi and the god's deciding vote to exonerate the mother-slaying Orestes–describe the conquest of the feminine principle. Her most targeted source, however, is Christian mythology. She draws from Joseph Campbell to reinterpret Christian myths in an ecofeminist vein. Although her expressed use of Campbell is confined to his concept of "syncretism" (which refers to both the polytheistic and monotheistic aspects of the Goddess) and his theory concerning the relationship between the Mother Goddess and the virgin Mary, she assimilates his understanding of the relationship between Jesus and the ancient mystery religions. Her "gylanic Christ" (whose myths and teachings emphasize a balance between feminine and masculine principles) fits the mold of a Mother Goddess satellite/son whose death and resurrection, as Campbell so clearly delineates, represents the archetypal quality of the myths concerned with nature's eternal cycle of birth and death as worshipped in the ancient mystery/fertility cults–the difference being that Christianity historized the rebirth of Jesus and made it a one-time event.

Convinced that the church fathers perverted the mythology and teachings of Jesus (which helped "to justify the Church's later androcratic structure and goals"), Eisler proclaims that Jesus' message was gylanic:

> He preached universal love and taught that the meek, humble, and weak would some day inherit the earth. Beyond this, in both his words and actions he often rejected the subservient and separate position that his culture assigned women. Freely associating with women, which was itself a form of heresy in his time, Jesus proclaimed the spiritual equality of all.[8]

Claiming that many scholars have recognized the ecofeminist, gylanic aspects of Jesus' teachings, Eisler insists that the antipatriarchal interpretation of his message represents a theological version of the new paradigm.

Indicative of her new-paradigm conviction, she suggests that Fritjof Capra's and Theodore Roszak's work and success reflect the West's move toward a more advanced version of a partnership society.[9] The ecofeminist awareness, which she contends ties her work with Capra's and Roszak's, is inevitable if androcratic dominance is to be transformed into a gylanic-centered, new-paradigm way of life.

III

THE REVITALIZATION OF THE DIONYSUS/SHIVA/YIN IMPULSE: CONCLUSIONS CONCERNING THE 1960S ZEITGEIST

> There is a revolution coming. It will not be like revolutions of the past. It will originate with the individual and with culture, and it will change the political structure only as its final act. It will not require violence to succeed, and it cannot be successfully resisted by violence. . . . This is the revolution of the new generation. . . . At the heart of everything is what we shall call a change of consciousness. This means a 'new head'—a new way of living—a new man. This is what the new generation has been searching for, and what it has started achieving.[1]

New-paradigm scholars describe the aims and effects of the 1960s revolution as the awakening of communal-consciousness. Charles Reich in *The Greening of America* insists that this awakening will incite a deeper commitment to love and wisdom. Communally liberating consciousness from the bonds of patriarchal, technocratic ways of thinking by opening the mystical, ecstatic realms of the unconscious, the countercultural youth have awakened and spread the experience of oneness between the self, community, and nature. In so doing, Reich indicates, they have made it clear that the Western individual "once more can become a creative force, renewing and creating his own life and thus giving life back to his society."[2] Fritjof Capra, who regards the concept "the sixties" as a state of consciousness which originated in the fifties and included the seventies, contends that this state is characterized by the transcendence of the ego through the communal psychic expansion which briefly fused the psychedelic experience with transpersonal psychology.

This state also established an awareness of communal power—power realized by peace and civil rights activists, women's rights groups, and environmentally concerned citizens. The creation of a broader understanding and experience of community has been, Theodore Roszak submits, the counterculture's psychic task. Ultimately, the revolutionary goal is to expand self-awareness toward a biospheric community.

Many communities—embodied by, for instance, African-Americans, Amerindians, women, peace activists, environmentalists, college students, and hippies—revolted in the sixties. The forms of the revolt involved activities such as riots, demonstrations, and festivals. Beginning in the seventies the principles behind the forms were articulated in ideologies such as Afrocentricity, Amerindian Earth Wisdom, feminism, and ecology. A province of new-paradigm scholarship, this articulation has provided a framework for digesting and expanding the alternative ideas and values practiced in the sixties. The articulation has shown how the transformation of consciousness has spread countercultural sensibilities by promoting ecological awareness and human/animal/planetary rights; propagating a pantheistic religion which includes such diverse perspectives as Eastern philosophy, Mother Earth worship, the findings of the new physics, and a re-mythologized Jesus Christ; inspiring the Greens, a new political party; initiating transpersonal psychology, a new study of the psyche; engendering new kinds of academic institutions (e.g., Esalen); and revelling in a Dionysian aesthetic (e.g., Beat literature, rock-and-roll music, and feminist films).

Slaves and victims of the system from the rise of the United States to the empowerment of its capitalistic-driven technocracy, African-Americans and Amerindians led revolutions based on communal-consciousness awakenings. "Black consciousness," "Black power," and "Black awareness"—slogans of the African-American revolution—have been articulated in terms of Afrocentricity. An evolving state of consciousness, Afrocentricity is the challenge that African-American culture has established in response to Eurocentrism and oppression in the United States. According to Molefi Asante, Afrocentricity means that "a new perspective, a new approach, a new consciousness pervades our behavior and consequently with Afrocentricity you see the movies differently, you see other people differently, you read books differently, you see politicians differently; in fact, nothing is as it was before your consciounsess. Your conversion to Afrocentricity becomes total as you read, listen, and talk with others who share the collective consciousness."[3] Representing a return to black roots, to African ancestory, history and mythology, tribal religions and rituals, fashions and names, and song and customs, Afrocentricity clarifies the black cause. At the same time it unites all humans in the challenge to create an egalitarian society–to culturally transform. The "transforming power which helps us to capture the true sense of our souls," Afrocentricity emphasizes that race is a political concept, not "a biological or anthropological fact," and that real activism entails engaging "our collective will to peace and consciousnesss."[4]

Spurred by the African-American revolution, Amerindians collectively began raising their voices and taking revolutionary action. Perfect examples are the "Red Power" battle cry and the seizure of Alcatraz in 1969 by a group who called themselves "All Indian Tribes." Unlike the African-Americans who, through (for instance) music and sports, attained a place in mainstream culture, the Amerindians have always been a counterculture. They were not only forced to exist on reservations governed by a military regime, the Amerindians were denied the means to interconnect tribally and to integrate in any meaningful way with United States culture–that is, until they took their cue from the Black Protest movement.

Only recently has the Amerindian way of life received the recognition it richly deserves. One of the reasons for the deepened appreciation is because the Earth Wisdom practiced by Indians for millenia found proponents in groups such as college students, ecologists, and feminists. The awareness of the sacredness of nature, so crucial to Amerindian culture, has not only fueled the recognition of their human rights, it–along with the African-American communal-consciousness awakening–has played an immense role in the evolution of the human rights movement to the rights of the planet.

Perhaps the most encompassing communal-consciousness awakening involved the youth's counterculture. It was encompassing in three major ways. First, the hippies and countercultural students were by and large the sons and daughters of corporate America; hence, they brought their anti-establishment discourse back home. Second, their notion of communal-consciousness incorporated all non-violent causes aimed at derailing technocracy. Third, the counterculture has had the most influence in creating and spreading a communal consciousness which stresses the connection between the self and cosmos. The hippies did not, of course, live a utopic life-style or create a model community. Many of their communal endeavors constituted perversions. From superficial interpretations of Eastern philosophy (e.g., using the *Kama Sutra* to support their free-love attitude) to countless drug overdoses, the excessively ecstasy-oriented nature of, for instance, the hippies cannot be ignored. However, if Roszak is right, the spirituality *behind* the sixties uninhibited sexuality, drug use, fashion, music, and rituals may provide "the saving vision our endangered civilization requires."[5] In other words, the incompleteness of the forms of the revolt in no way detracts from the significance of the principles which characterized the revolution. Or, as Reich alleges, "the whole emerging pattern, from ideals to campus demonstrations to beads and bell bottoms to the Woodstock Festival, makes sense and is part of a consistent philosophy."[6] The consistency of this philosophy is derived from its pantheistic center–i.e., the belief that the divine exists in all things. In short, the communal-consciousness awakening which gave rise to the counterculture also gave rise to the renewal of a very ancient pantheistic spirituality.

Ecology and feminism are the two movements which scholars associate most often with sixties consciousness and new-paradigm spirituality. Ecology has existed as a science since the beginning of this century, but it was the sixties that disseminated a mass awareness of its spiritual dimension–namely, the feminine principle, Mother Earth. That the allegiance between ecology and feminism rests on this principle is not surprising because, as all contemporary new-paradigm scholars observe, the patriarchal West has always identified woman with nature.

The movements not only share a common antagonist, patriarchal consciousness, but a common pantheistic philosophy—as Capra notes: "Feminist spirituality is based on awareness of the oneness of all living forms and of their cyclical rhythms of birth and death, thus reflecting an attitude toward life that is profoundly ecological."[7] This attitude is also explicit, as Roszak maintains, in the goal to revive the awareness of nature's sacredness:

> Clearly, there are those among us, at least in the women's movement, who recognize the ecological emergency of our time for the profound spiritual failure it is. They know we are not going to save ourselves with a quick technological fix and more efficient resource management. Rather, the Goddess is going to have to be reborn in our midst, not simply as a systems analyst's hypothesis, but as living culture.[8]

Despite the fact that ecology and feminism share the same spiritual aim (to supplant the West's dominion-over-nature attitude with a renewed reverence for nature), unique interpretations of their respective ideologies have caused a variety of controversies. One of the most profound controversies exists between ecofeminism and deep ecology. While deep ecologists regard the neo-pagan vein in ecofeminism as a form of New Age occultism, ecofeminists argue that deep ecologists' failure to integrate feminist concerns in their political platform leaves their movement androcentric or merely a refined version of patriarchal control. This controversy, which has existed for over a decade, has carried both positive and negative effects—effects which Robert Sessions, in "Deep Ecology versus Ecofeminism: Healthy Differences or Incompatible Philosophies?," addresses:

> On the positive side, many thinkers from these two camps have helped each other understand better their own views and those they oppose, and they have deepened their own and our understanding of the difficult issues we face. In contrast, some of the exchanges have been rather rancorous: some deep ecologists have accused ecofeminism of shallowness, anthropocentrism, short sightedness, and environmental naivete, while various ecofeminists have called their accusers sexist, shallow, ahistorical, stoical, and even fascist.[9]

The disagreements between ecological- and feminist-based groups reflect the difficulty in unifying countercultural sensibilities. However, on a deeper level, they also expose the need for such a unification because "the difficult issues we face" are of a spiritual nature which necessarily fuse the goals of both camps. Arne Naess–who coined the term "deep ecology"–suggests, "A total view, such as deep ecology, can provide a single motivating force for all the activities and movements aimed at saving the planet from human exploitation and domination."[10] Naess's use of the phrase "such as" is crucial because the term ecofeminism is, in this all-encompassing sense, interchangeable with the term deep ecology.

Reflective of the Zeitgeist that fueled the ideologies of deep ecologists and ecofeminists, various forms of a new aesthetic impulse emerged in the fifties and sixties. Two very pronounced examples of this radically new aesthetic spirit surfaced in beat literature and Rock music. Jack Kerouac, the beat king, not only coined the term "beat generation," he captured it in his novels. He also captured its failures–in particular, the perversions involving communal sex, the use of drugs, and the popularization of Eastern thought. In *Zen and the Art of Motorcycle Maintenance* Robert Pirsig presents us with a more sophisticated depiction of the new values practiced in the 1960s. By contrasting the values embodied by the characters in Kerouac's *Dharma Bums* with those expressed by the protagonist in Pirsig's *Zen*, Chapter Eleven determines how the forms of the sixties revolt evolved into the principles of change which the revolt fostered. The aim, in other words, is to examine the way in which the revolution was embodied, digested, critiqued, and systematized in terms of the new paradigm. My aim in Chapter Twelve is to do the same with Rock music: to show how rock-and-roll artists channelled the forms of the music's rebellious aspects into expressions of a new worldview based on the Dionysus/Shiva/yin impulse. In other words, the final two chapters examine manifestations of the aesthetic impulse (one literary and the other musical) of the sixties Zeitgeist which reject the West's reason-as-virtue paradigm that has suppressed the cultivation of the feminine, ecological aspects of human nature for over two thousand years.

11

The Meeting of East, West, and the Sixties Eros: *Dharma Bums* and *Zen and the Art of Motorcycle Maintenance*

> . . . a lot of people say he [Christ] is Maitreya, the Buddha prophesied to appear after Sakyamuni, you know, Maitreya means 'love' in Sanskrit and that's all Christ talked about was love. . . . Think what a great world revolution will take place when East meets West finally, and it'll be guys like us that can start the thing.[1]

The 1960s Zeitgeist opened doors to all kinds of love. Free love, universal love, Jesus love (as proclaimed by "freaks"), bhakti-devotion (as practiced by Krishna Kids), and Dionysian ecstasy are catch phrases for the unconventional types of love propagated mainly by American and European youth of the sixties. These unconventional expressions of love, generated by the beats and cultivated by the hippies, were openly opposed to the values of society. Besides the sexually explicit music and the use of mind-expanding drugs, a very significant element in the counterculture's revolt was the adaptation of Eastern philosophy as a means to attempt to establish and legitimize unconventional ways of loving. Jack Kerouac's *Dharma Bums* (1958) and Robert Pirsig's *Zen and the Art of Motorcycle Maintenance* (1974) portray, respectively, this adaptation in its grass roots and its philosophical culmination. In other words, Kerouac's depiction of the beat lifestyle (particularly the orgies, intoxication, and anti-intellectualism) marks a return to Dionysian forms, whereas Pirsig's message represents a return to Dionysian principles which are based on self-understanding or finding the demon within.

In a manner indicative of the established society's evaluation of hippie modes of love, a professor of medicine and President of the New York State Council on Drug Addiction, Donald Louria, claimed that although hippies incessantly talk about love, they are quite incapable of conventionally accepting or giving love.[2] Regarding the hippie notion of universal love as mere hallucinogenic-created illusion and hippies' uninhibited sexuality as senseless perversion, social institutions and authorities did their best to devalue all aspects of the counterculture's unconventionality. However, they were unsuccessful for significant reasons–as Pirsig explains: the cultural changes begun in the sixties are "still in the process of reshaping our whole national outlook on things. The 'generation gap' has been a result of it. The names 'beat' and 'hip' grew out of it. Now it's become apparent that this dimension isn't a fad that's going to go away next year or the year after. It's here to stay because it's a very serious and important way of looking at things."[3] In other words, behind the rebellious aspects of beat and hippie conceptions of love exists an important alternative to Western culture's value system. This challenge, as portrayed in *Dharma Bums* and *Zen,* is directed at society's neglect of eros and its exaltation of reason (logos), law and order (nomos), and the Christian concept of love (agape) based on the grace of a transcendent God. These three concepts–logos, nomos, and agape–have proven to be the cornerstones of the Western value system which the eros-driven counterculture not only rejected, but, if new-paradigm scholars prove right, is transforming.

In both Greek philosophy and Judeo-Christian theology, logos and nomos have various meanings. However, in a generic philosophical and theological sense, logos refers to the divine mind which, discernible through human reason, accounts for the intelligible structure of the universe; nomos is the cosmic law emanating from this mind. Agape, on the other hand, is a New Testament concept denoting God's unconditional gift of love to man. Each of these concepts contributes to the metaphysical constitution of conventional love: logos, affiliated with the Socratic virtue-as-knowledge edict, exemplifies the Western world's reverence of reason, science, and technology; nomos accounts for the high value accorded institutions of law, legal contracts, and religious doctrine; and agape represents pure spiritual love which flows from God to humans—who, ideally, share it with others.

The unconventional love of beats and hippies, in its highest form, can be described as eros. Eros represents the urge to unite, or, nature's principle of creative attraction manifest in humans as the tendency toward physical and spiritual fusion of lover/subject and beloved/object. In *The Nature of Sympathy*, Max Scheler describes eros as "the sense of cosmic unity in all its forms . . . the quintessential depth of life itself—the daemonic element, as it were, that lies within." Scheler maintains that the West has fallen out of touch with eros. Although he was writing in the early part of the century, his attack on the "relatively normal world-outlook" reflects many of the aims which characterize the sixties revolt in terms of the relationship between eros and society's logos/nomos/agape-oriented value system. Scheler regards the Judeo-Christian "doctrine of God as the invisible spiritual 'Lord and Maker' of the world" as the destructive agency of the Greek eros because God's transcendence makes "the whole of Nature . . . vastly less animate and less alive, while man as a spiritual being is given such decided precedence over Nature that all feeling for unity with Nature is branded as paganism for centuries afterwards." Between Christianity and the advancement of science, the West has created a "one-sided conception of Nature as a mere instrument of human domination." What Friedrich Nietzsche calls the "devilization" (*Verteufelung*) of eros, Scheler regards as beliefs "which have undermined the foundations of our sense of unity with the living cosmos."[4] Both agree that the West has rationally dissected and dissipated the spirit of eros, thus perverting the sacredness of our relationship to nature. A reunification with eros is only possible, Scheler persists, through the cultivation of a new worldview—one that depicts nature as an intrinsically qualitative being rather than an aggregation of usable quantities.

In their respective, aforementioned novels, both Kerouac and Pirsig attempt to revive Western man's awareness of his sacred bond to nature. The authors' means of doing so are very similar. While attacking society's overemphasis on reason, law, order, control and its neglect of intuition, imagination, creativity, and spontaneity, Kerouac and Pirsig develop a culture-versus-nature theme in which logos, nomos, and agape are juxtaposed with eros. Both novels are autobiographical confessionals and involve travelling across America–where busy, goal-oriented people in cities run around without any sense of the here and now while the protagonist, undergoing an odyssey into the deeper, darker self, constantly communes with nature. Both use Eastern thought to extol eros and expose the limits of conventional love. The metaphor of mountain-climbing as a spiritual journey toward erotic self-realization also unites the books' themes.

Despite these similarities, however, the purported ends are quite different. Kerouac's characters break with all kinds of social conventions; but, much like the beat movement itself, their revolt is aimless–based mostly on uninhibited sex, the use of drugs, and the propagation of a curious mixture of Eastern philosophy. Pirsig (who is the main character of *Zen*) seeks to balance the values associated with science and religion, nature and culture, eros and logos/nomos/agape, the philosophy of East and West. Pirsig's book also challenges cultural value assumptions but offers what he considers to be a more serious alternative than those of the hippies–who, he contends, offered only colorful, short-term alternatives which "were looking more and more like pure degeneracy."[5]

In *The Making of a Counter Culture*, Theodore Roszak accuses Kerouac and the beats of the same type of degeneracy: "Kerouac's brand of modish Zen, Watts gently criticized, '. . . confuses "anything goes" at the existential level with "anything goes" at the artistic and social levels.'"[6] Although this is, in essence, a fair criticism, it should be tempered with the understanding that the free love, drugs, and attitudes of anti-war, -materialism, -oppression, -tradition of Kerouac represent the brash beginnings of a new awareness, an awareness which would proliferate in mass proportions. As William Everson asserts in his article "Dionysus and the Beat Generation," "the Beat Generation is perhaps the most significant American example of a universal trend: the reemergence in the twentieth century of the Dionysian spirit."[7] Roszak regards the beats' adaptation of Zen—despite their crude simplifications—as indicative of this spirit: "If the young seized on Zen with shallow understanding, they grasped it with a healthy instinct . . . the spontaneous urge to counter the joyless, rapacious, and egomaniacal order of our technological society."[8]

Through the different perspectives of his protagonists, Kerouac presents a diffusion of Eastern thought: although Japhy Ryder (Kerouac's friend, Gary Snyder) remains true to his nihilistic, ecstatic Zen, Ray Smith (the narrator/Kerouac) mixes his cosmic-, service-oriented Mahayana Buddhism with elements of Christianity and Ryder's Zen. Despite inevitable philosophical incoherences (which do not necessarily detract from Kerouac's aesthetic aims), there is no question that his use of Eastern thought promotes an unconventional worldview. His characterization of Ryder, the acclaimed ultimate Dharma Bum, is a perfect example of his rejection of logos/nomos in favor of eros. For instance, Princess claims, "Besides all the background he has, in Oriental scholarship, Pound, taking peyote and seeing visions, his mountainclimbing and bhikkuing, wow, Japhy Ryder is a great new hero of American culture." Smith also clearly juxtaposes and justifies Ryder's erotic nature over and against society's logos/nomos norms in his claim that the masses live "in rows of well-to-do houses with lawns and television sets in each living room with everybody looking at the same thing and thinking the same thing at the same time while the Japhies of the world go prowling in the wilderness to hear the voice crying in the wilderness . . . ."[9]

Kerouac's anti-logos theme is manifest most explicitly in his adaptation of Buddhism. Using Buddhism, he attempts to devalue technocracy's emphasis on the intellect by claiming that ultimate truth not only eludes rational explication, reason is a hindrance to its attainment. In Smith's world, logos refers to the suppressive power of reason while nomos equals mere convention because laws discovered or created by the intellect are man-made illusions, part of the ineffable void.

Kerouac also attacks nomos in terms of society's written and unwritten laws regarding sexual love. What Ryder suggests that he and his friends are doing in their version of the Tibetan "yabyum sex rites" is celebrating the sex instinct as divine, as a means to participate in the spiritual realm. For instance, Princess, who enters the story with a rock-and-roll artist, rationalizes her participation in the rites as part of her process of becoming a bodhisattva and her fulfilling her dharma as "the old mother of earth": "I feel like I'm the mother of all things and I have to take care of my little children."[10] Although one cannot help but sense a perversion here, Scheler does describe the sexual act in terms of the erotic union of two partners conspiring to touch "the eternal Mother of all things living." On the other hand, as Roszak suggests: "Again, this looks very much like postwar middle-class permissiveness reaching out for a religious sanction, finding it, and making the most of it."[11] Although Kerouac's characters (much like the beats and hippies) do not offer any solutions or even insights into Western society's sexual "hang-ups"—what Scheler calls the West's "metaphysical degradation of the sexual act"—they seem to know against what (or whom) they are revolting. In Scheler's words:

> Virtually all the customs and institutions, and the whole climate of sexual and erotic life in the West, show a . . . dominance of Mechanism. . . . this mechanistic viewpoint is by no means confined to any particular intellectual group, such as are formed by churches, sects and political parties, or by groupings of a professional, social or class character. For it is the hallmark of *bourgeois man, homo capitalisticus*, who is to be found in all these groups.[12]

According to Scheler, one of the imperatives to a reunification with eros is to restore the idea of the sexual act to its true metaphysical significance. In other words, society needs to liberate the sexual act from the Judeo-Christian teleological ethics which suppress the innate sacredness of the act by attributing its entire value to its purported end, namely, reproduction. The sexual act, as an experience celebrating and fusing with the creative life force of nature, contains within itself its value and purpose. Although Kerouac's characters do revolt against the conventional mores concerning sex, they fail to elevate sex in any meaningful way. Instead, they justify having sex with any partner because they regard it as a mere instrument of ecstatic transcendence. Ryder rejects all philosophies and social systems that in any way villify sex and feels free to use sex whenever he feels like "amusing himself in the void." Naively, Ryder lumps together all Eastern philosophies concerning sex in order to rationalize his lifestyle, claiming that the freedom regarding sex was one of the aspects that attracted him to Eastern religion. Smith, who is having problems balancing his undefined morality and the "Zen Free Love Lunacy orgies" of Ryder, is not sure at all what to do about the question of sex. Until the escapades with Princess, he had practiced a year of celibacy (as Kerouac purportedly had before writing *Dharma Bums*) because–at that point–he felt sex was cruel and offensive. Admittedly, Smith changed his mind frequently. In *Jack Kerouac: Prophet of the New Romanticism*, Robert Hipkiss concisely sums up Kerouac's failure: "The quest for ecstasy on the part of the Kerouac heroes overshadows ideals of human responsiblity and love."[13] Kerouac, perhaps aware of the inadequacy of his position, has Smith say, "'Poor gentle flesh,' I realized, 'there is no answer.'"[14]

Kerouac's portrayal of eros/Eastern philosophy also suffers from superficiality in the mystical realm. For instance, Smith haphazardly interchanges Ryder's Buddha/void and his own strange mixture of Christianity's and Mahayana Buddhism's God/ultimate reality. Smith admits his confusion to Ryder: "I felt suppressed by this schism we have about separating Buddhism and Christianity, East from West, what the hell difference does it make? We're all in Heaven now, aint we?"[15] Roszak justifiably equates Kerouac's adaptation of Buddhism with "Timothy Leary's brand of easy-do syncretism: 'somehow' all is one–but never mind precisely how."[16] Hipkiss, agreeing with Watts, claims that Kerouac "tends to ignore the 'conventional limits of human community' and to blur the distinctions of good and evil by viewing human life from the 'ultimate standpoint.'"[17] The point is, although Kerouac's adulterated conglomeration of Eastern thought enables him to plug into an established, yet, to the West, unconventional worldview, the result is a revolt pervaded with superficiality.

Despite its weaknesses, Kerouac's *Dharma Bums* offers an insightful dramatization of the beats' eros in its direct opposition to a love originating from a purely transcendent God. Always careful not to degrade Christianity, Smith supplants the notion of God's gift of love, agape, with the cultivation of the love within. In Hipkiss's words: "In Kerouac's work the key to love is complete acceptance of everything as Divine."[18] In Smith's words:

> Here, this, is It. The world as it is, is Heaven, I'm looking for a Heaven outside what there is, it's only this poor pitiful world that's heaven. Ah, if I could realize, if I could forget myself and devote my meditations to the freeing, the awakening and the blessedness of all living creatures everywhere I'd realize what there is, is ecstasy.[19]

This ecstatic understanding is Smith's goal. Kerouac unveils Smith's self-realization process by interrelating the metaphors of mountains as Buddha-nature and being on or climbing mountains as a spiritual journey. Smith is involved in two adventures on mountains–one with Ryder and Morely and the other by himself (as a summer lookout for the forest service). Early in their ascent, Smith follows Ryder step for step. However, taking Japhy's advice that he must create his own Zen dance up the mountain, he does not take long to learn that it is best to forge his own path. Smith and Ryder concur that the secret to climbing rests in the recognition that each step leads the climber closer to self-realization. Free of the monotonous conventions of society's "flat ground" reality, the goal, Japhy implies, is obvious: "to me a mountain is a Buddha."[20]

The summit of Smith's self-actualization occurs on his last day on Desolation Mountain (on the last page of the book) when, filled with the sadness of returning to the city, he proclaims his love for God. Although this is another example of Smith's fusion of a personal God with his notion of Buddha, his reaching out from within is clearly erotic. Moreover, it is in direct opposition to agape. As Anders Nygren claims in *Agape and Eros*, "Eros is an upward movement" and "Agape comes down. Eros is man's way to God" and "agape is God's way to man. Eros is man's effort: it assumes that man's salvation is his own work." Agape, on the other hand, "is God's grace: salvation is the work of Divine love."[21] In short, Smith's spiritual journey ends with the ecstatic acceptance of the divine in all things.

Dharma Bums represents the beat movement: a revolt without answers. In place of logos, Kerouac offers unbridled emotion; for nomos, he offers chaos and anarchy; and for agape, a perverted sense of eros. Even though Smith recognizes the divine in all things, there does not seem to be any sense in which he shows any signs of self-betterment. For instance, early in the book, Smith claims that even before he met Ryder, "I was a perfect Dharma Bum myself." Moreover, even on his first mountain climb, where Smith was the novice, Morley claims that Smith was "the smartest of them all."[22] The point is, Kerouac uses, but perverts, eros and Eastern philosophy in his attack on social values. As Hipkiss claims, Kerouac and his characters end "stranded between an unsatisfactory world and an untenable heaven, somewhere in the void."[23]

With the sixties as hindsight ("a decade in which reason has been assailed and assaulted beyond the wildest beliefs of the fifties"), Pirsig develops a much more sophisticated attack on society's over-evaluation of nomos and logos and its neglect of eros.[24] He not only confronts rather than avoids society's institutionalization of logos and nomos, he suggests ways to circumvent it. Moreover, his approach is much more conventional. For instance, unlike the series of events involving Kerouac's ecstatically obsessed characters, *Zen* is the story of a father-son relationship through which the father overcomes his insane, reason-obsessed self of the past. It is based on Pirsig's 1968 motorcycle trip with his son, Chris, and his reflections on the nature of his own insanity, which led to shock treatments in 1961. As R. Z. Sheppard observes, "To give his philosophical inquiries a dramatic edge, Pirsig refers to his shadowy pre-treatment self as Phaedrus, the name of one of Socrates' straight men from Plato's *Dialogues*."[25]

Pirsig sets the stage for the eros versus logos/nomos theme early in the book: he, Chris, and two friends, John and Sylvia, are riding their motorcycles on an old highway to avoid the tensions of the expressway, to feel closer to nature, and to be able to stop in country towns, where people are kinder and more in touch with the hereness and nowness of things. They have no time-table to follow, no particular place to go (except that the mountains are their goal), and simply "want to make good time, but for us now this is measured with emphasis on 'good' rather than 'time' and when you make that shift in emphasis the whole

ZAMM ↓ 115

approach changes."[26] Pirsig begins his musings complaining about the hang-ups that John and Sylvia (whom he associates with beatnik, hippie, and antisystems people) have regarding technology. He realizes that their problem is shared by masses of people and that it has resulted from the wall that the West has built between reason and passion, fact and value. He addresses the dilemma through his recognition of two worlds: the romantic and the classical. The romantic world is conceived through an imaginative, intuitive, and creative mode of thought while the classical understanding of the world is based on reason and laws. Pirsig's attack is directed at the theoretical separation of these two worlds, which he insists were put into conflict by the Western world's general acceptance of Plato's and Aristotle's theories.

Although his philosophy–which he expounds as Chautauguas intended to edify and entertain–also suffers from superficiality, Pirsig's message is insightful: to bridge the gap between eros and logos/nomos, between Eastern and Western philosophy, between religious mysticism and scientific positivism, the West needs to reevaluate its understanding of and assumptions concerning the relationship of intuition and reason, creativity and order, spontaneity and control, and, most importantly, quality and quantity.[27] The solution, ultimately, is to recognize individually and to concur collectively that the goal of all activity is Quality (which Pirsig equates with the Buddha and the Tao). In terms of human experience, he refers to Quality as a well-balanced, tuned-in state of mind. It is care, enthusiasm, and stillness magically wrapped in one. It is characterized by one's being into whatever one is doing, whether meditating, fixing something, or fishing. Quality disintegrates all forms of anxiety, boredom, impatience, and ego-attachments.

As the inner source of gumption and peace of mind, Quality is eros. It represents the ability, drawn from the inner self, to determine what is good. This knowledge represents the culmination of what Pirsig attempts to describe as Quality, care, eros, or love. "The Greeks called it *enthousiasmos*, the root of 'enthusiasm,' which means literally 'filled with theos,' or God, or Quality."[28] By recognizing the divine within, one transcends subject-object dichotomies and identifies with the very source of

Quality. Because traditional rationality divides the world into parts, it relegates Quality, a holistic phenomenon, to a meaningless, irrational realm of human endeavor. Hence, it is self-knowledge that enables one to see the fallacies of society's value assumptions which glorify reason and degrade eros.

Pirsig depicts his own self-actualization in his gradual coming-to-grips with the ghost of Phaedrus and the ghost of rationality itself. He attempts to understand Phaedrus's obsession by reading his fragments and pondering what went wrong. He comes to the conclusion that Phaedrus's logic-breaking realization and consequent intellectual dilemma stemmed from his awareness that the rational methodology which began with Plato's dialogues and culminated in Aristotle's classification and categorization of everything left out the heart of ancient Greek *arete*. He quotes H. D. F. Kitto: "Arete implies a respect for the wholeness or oneness of life, and a consequent dislike of specialization."[29] Kitto also explains that in Plato, arete is translated as virtue; however, a better translation is excellence. For Phaedrus, "Lightning hits! Quality! Virtue! Dharma!" They are one and the same: an essence which cannot be broken down. Definitions do not fit. Quality transcends rational perception because it exists prior to any subjects or objects—"facts do not exist until value has created them." Humans conceive reality thinking that they are merely perceiving it. It is on the basis of Quality that we perceive/conceive reality. Yet Plato and Aristotle subordinated Quality to reason. One of the many consequences of their success has been the separation of Western technology from *techne* (which is the Greek word for art). That is, technology developed "the tendency to do what is 'reasonable' even when it isn't any good."[30] That, according to Pirsig, was Phaedrus's realization of the heart of the problem.

In an attempt to overcome this problem, Phaedrus created a new spiritual rationality in which "the spiritual blankness of dualistic technological reason would become illogical. Reason was no longer to be 'value free.' Reason was to be subordinate, logically, to Quality."[31] To achieve the marriage of reason and quality, Phaedrus promoted a Church of Reason and argued that he had found the bridge between the classical and romantic worlds. Here, Pirsig claims, was Phaedrus's mistake: he did not see that reason and quality are helplessly antithetical.

Armed with this insight, Pirsig was ready to bury Phaedrus forever. He not only reintegrates himself socially, he develops a new dimension in his ability to love. Aware of the power of eros and no longer obsessed with rationally understanding it, Pirsig asserts that a cultural transformation will have to begin individually, with caring people getting in touch with Quality.

In his promotion of eros and his reevaluation of logos, Pirsig adopts his own conglomerate version of Eastern thought. He fuses Hinduism, Buddhism, and Taoism, claiming that the basic doctrine of all three centers on the *tat tvam asi* ("Thou art that") truth. He points to Zen meditation as the perfect example of a way to break down rationality's subject-object dichotomy because it aims at procuring direct contact with truth without differentiating between the self and the environment. Zen does not aim at intellectual understanding; rather, it attempts to confound and exhaust the intellect to the point that its boundaries are exposed and the realization of another, less-confining type of awareness becomes manifest. By repeatedly confronting the intellect with transrational stimuli, Zen provokes out of conceptual understanding an experiential realization. Hence, "logos, the root word of 'logic' . . . the sum total of our rational understanding of the world," is something to be overcome in the process of self-actualization.[32]

Phaedrus's problem was that he was a logos-dominated person. He admitted that no matter how hard he tried, he could not understand F. S. C. Northrop's *The Meeting of East and West* because of his inability to let go of his Western mind-set. He suffered from maintaining what Northrop calls "a philosophy of life which shuts its eyes to the creative fire in man's nature, to the eros or frenzy in all its human manifestations"; hence, he cut his "soul off from the fresh, warm bodily, earthly feeling of life and from the emotional, aesthetic and spiritual component of man's nature" and became "artificial, stereotyped, without individuality of the feelings, sentiments and imagination, afraid of . . . emotions, tense, and . . . colorless and neurotic."[33]

Hand in hand with his reevaluation of logos, Pirsig condemns society's deification of nomos. He complains that "institutions such as schools, churches, governments and political organizations of every sort all tended to direct thought for ends other than truth, for the perpetuation of their own functions, and for control of individuals in the service of these functions." In other words, the Western world's obsession with law, order, and control sublimated the forces of eros. Again, he offers Quality as a solution to the rational mayhem: "A real understanding of Quality captures the System, tames it, and puts it to work for one's personal use, while leaving one completely free to fulfill his inner destiny."[34]

There is no doubt that Pirsig's philosophy suffers from incoherencies and inconsistencies. However, because his approach is aesthetic and his intentions are spiritual, to aim at a rigorous philosophical justification of his thought is to miss the point. Along with making a thorough and honest attempt to expose the reasons for the Western world's promotion of logos and nomos and its neglect of eros, he preaches the value in creating a balance between them. Unlike Kerouac, Pirsig not only captures the "irrational elements crying for assimilation that creates the present bad quality, the chaotic disconnected spirit of the twentieth century," he applies the positive elements of the sixties, including the meeting of East and West, in his development of a holistic worldview. While explaining the incredible commercial success of *Zen*, Pirsig calls it a "culture-bearer." "Culture-bearing books challenge cultural value assumptions and often do so at a time when the culture is changing in favor of their challenge."[35] If *Zen* is a culture-bearer, *Dharma Bums* is a counterculture-bearer—or, what Kerouac helped create, Pirsig sought to bring to a climax.

12

Rock-and-Roll's Twist and Shout for Dionysus

> Rock's primitivism is a compulsion whose happy victims are beyond rational control. In myth at least no one chooses to be a rocker, any more than Pentheus chooses to follow Dionysos.[1]

Phenomena originating some three thousand years apart, Dionysianism and rock-and-roll shared ritual similarities which generated common patterns of revolt, protest, and assimilation into culture. Aspects of the group-possessing rituals included music, dance, sex, drugs, and lyrics. The common pattern of revolt/protest centered on the way the worship of nature, emotion, spontaneity, sexuality, and unity by the devotees of each cult evolved from an unconscious revolt against to a conscious protest of the reason-, control-, and order-oriented value systems dominant in patriarchal society. While the Greek bacchantes (also called Thyiades, or "wild women") practiced the revolt's forms in the oreibasia, a later Dionysian rite, the dithyramb, provided the underclasses with a means of protest and planted the seeds of drama. In America, the youth of the 1950s and early 1960s united in rock-and-roll's anti-establishment forms which were aimed and intensified by the counterculture of the middle to late sixties.[2] This transformation became possible in both Greece and America when artists began to use their lyrics to confront existential and social issues, to express values, and to generate change. In so doing, they turned the forms into principles and the cultic impulses into aesthetic forces of their respective mainstream societies. Together, as the first part of this chapter shows, the mass intoxicating rituals, the sophistication of the lyrics, and the popularization of the protesters' aims demonstrate how Dionysianism and rock-and-roll embodied their respective Zeitgeists.

The second part of this chapter, while expanding upon the artists' aims, interprets rock-and-roll's new-paradigm values as expressed in recurring messages–involving themes such as pantheism, Eastern philosophy, and ecological awareness–in commercially successful and/or mass-appreciated rock-and-roll songs.[3] In other words, after examining how rock-and-roll revitalized Dionysianism in practice, I intend to elucidate how the increasingly sophisticated messages in rock-and-roll songs serve as, if not the most significant, certainly the loudest voice of the 1960s counterculture.

The major common denominator of the first ritual similarity, the music, centers on the use of percussive and rhythm instruments as a source of group possession. While hand drums, rattles, castanets, and cymbals were central to the bacchantes' oreibasia and the later-developed dithyramb, the drums and amplified guitars are standard instruments of Rock bands. These instruments create the unrelenting beat and rhythm which serve as the driving, narcotic force behind both musics. Even the melody-producing instruments accentuate this force. The piercing sounds of the flute (aulos) were common to both the oreibasia and dithyramb, while the stringed cithara was also central to the dithyramb. Like rock-and-roll's rollicking solos on guitars, saxophones, amplified organs and microphoned pianos, Dionysian melodies were based on improvisations of a simple, repetitive theme and completely disengaged from a learned system of musical notation. For instance, after suggesting that the dithyramb originated in the worship of Dionysus, Plato describes its deviations from "fixed rules" of music:

> In course of time, an unmusical license set in with the appearance of poets who were men of native genius, but ignorant of what is right and legitimate in the realm of the Muses. Possessed by a frantic and unhallowed lust for pleasure, they contaminated laments with hymns and paeans with dithyrambs, actually imitated the strains of the flute on the harp, and created a universal confusion of forms.[4]

Plato complained that this unregimented use of the flute and cithara in the dithyramb resulted in the "divorce" of "rhythm and figure from melody" and that "the use of either as an independent instrument is no better than unmusical legerdemain."[5] While these "unmusical" elements of the dithyramb existed in the oreibasia, rock-and-roll owes much of its musical vitality to rhythm-and-blues.

Although various fields of music—such as ragtime, jazz, gospel, folk, blues, pop, and country-and-western—influenced rock-and-roll, the true precursor was rhythm-and-blues.[6] Besides its soul vocals (which I shall discuss later), it was characterized by heavy percussion and a driving rhythm, which is a direct descendant of tribal Africa's primitive musics.[7] While pop as well as country-and-western artists and audiences generally consisted of whites, rhythm-and-blues artists and audiences were predominantly black. Until 1950, the music business referred to rhythm-and-blues as "race music." As whites like Bill Haley, Jerry Lee Lewis, and Buddy Holly incorporated the rhythm-and-blues sound—not the vocals—into their music while casting off their country-and-western styles of music, it was Fats Domino, Bo Diddly, Little Richard, and Chuck Berry who fully captured and expressed these primitive elements. When asked to discuss the difference between rhythm-and-blues and rock-and-roll, Bo Diddley stated, "When we sang for black people, they called it rhythm and blues. When we sang the same songs for white people, they called it rock and roll. The audience was all that changed, not the music."[8]

The second ritual similarity, the dance, created group identity by communally fulfilling the possessive powers of the music. By the mid-fifties, to its cult members rock-and-roll dances meant a transcendence from a controlled, rather boring reality to a world of explosive, uninhibited fun. At parties, concerts, school and various activity-club functions, the young shook themselves into frenzies and the authorities into anti-frenzy frenzies. For adults the music was always too loud and the dance an obvious form of revolt. Although the terms of the revolt had not been established, right from the beginning, the public feared the possessive capabilities of rock-and-roll's music and dance. As John Orman reports in *The Politics of Rock Music*, Boston's Roman Catholic Church insisted that it be banned; the Encyclopaedia Britannica yearbook called it "insistent savagery"; adults around the country were calling it a Communist plot and/or the work of the Devil; an associate professor of psychiatry at Columbia University, A. M. Merrio, bluntly stated, "If we cannot stem the tide of rock and roll with its waves of rhythmic narcosis and of future waves of vicarious craze, we are preparing our downfall in the midst of pandemic funeral dances."[9]

Like the music, the dance is improvised. It consists in the individual's direct physical response to the music. However, the entire group and not just the partners share in this vigorously unstructured movement. The technique and aim of this individual/group effort is unlearned rather than learned, more shamanistic than romantic, sacred as opposed to profane. Clearly, rock-and-roll dance marks a return to orgiastic magic. In *The Triumph of Vulgarity*, Robert Pattison describes rock-and-roll dance as "the ritual celebration of the sentient self imitating the Dionysian infinity."[10] The youth united because they felt the same about their ecstatic experience and because the Apollonian generations could not relate. In short, while providing the youth with a group identity, the rite of music and dance also functioned as an unconscious revolt against and a spiritual liberation from patriarchal values.

The same can be said of the oreibasia and the dithyramb in regards to women and the lower classes, respectively. Frantically swirling in a circle around the dance/mime leader representing Dionysus, the bacchantes and dithyrambic satyrs worshipped sex–the third ritual similarity. While the bacchantes may have engaged in orgies, the drunken satyrs of the earliest dithyrambs wore large phalli which crudely portrayed Dionysus' sexual, life-giving power.[11] The movement in the dithy-ramb is related to the dance, tyrbasia, which apparently means "revolt," "revel," or "riot."[12] This tumultuous movement not only contradicted society's sexual mores, it helped spread mass sexual hysteria in the name of Dionysus.

Rock-and-roll dance spread the same kind of hysteria. While Mick Jagger and Jim Morrison are notable leaders of the Dionysian dance in the Rock realm, Elvis Presley ignited the hysteria. His ability to fuse rhythm-and-blues vocals in a commercially successful pop style along with his sexually expressive dance style made Presley rock-and-roll's first cultic idol. In his classic *Bomb Culture*, Jeff Nuttall accurately sums up why Elvis, the "supersalesman of mass-distribution hip," quickly transcended the huge image his business colleagues had planned for him:

> Most of all, he was unvarnished sex taken and set way out in the open. From the first quavering orgastic stutter to the final bull scream, from the first beads of sweat on his upper lip to the final frantic blows of his loins against the curved fetish of his guitar, he was the incarnate spirit of the fast lay, and his audience of adolescents responded, not only sexually but also with some gratitude, for here was someone who was acting out in the open something that was still a secret from the adults. He broke the secret and made himself a god all over the world.
>
> "God" is not too strong a word here. The Presley riots were a revengeful rediscovery of the Dionysian ceremony. He was the idol in a literal sense, a deity incarnate on the old primitive pattern, the catalyst of a rediscovered appetite for community in its fundamental form, orgastic ritual. Presley's success had implications far beyond the hopes or intentions of his managers and promoters. He was awarded an identity far greater than the one he intended for himself, an identity that invalidated the brash commercialism of his promotion.[13]

To the older generations, Presley personified sexual perversion. Shown from the waist up on his first Ed Sullivan appearance and forcibly instructed by police to sing while not moving at a concert in Florida, his dance style consistently resulted in a barrage of formal and informal accusations. For instance, while parents wrote letters of condemnation to TV and concert authorities after each of Presley's performances, a Los Angeles critic claimed that Elvis's gyrating pelvis was aimed at the "libidos" of "little girls" and a New York preacher called him the "whirling dervish of sex."[14] While effigies of him were hung and burned in different cities, to his idol worshipping fans, the original "teeny boppers," Presley's dance offered them an unconscious source of sexual freedom. The "love and fury" of these revelers, as George Melly aptly explains in *Revolt into Style*, did not begin with social "resentment as such, but something much more primitive; a religious impulse, the need to sacrifice the Godhead in order to elevate it above temporal considerations. And just because the overt emphasis is sexual rather than spiritual in no way invalidates this argument. Throughout history religious enthusiasm at this level is frequently indistinguishable from sexual hysteria."[15]

What Elvis mania suggested in the fifties was realized in the embrace of Eastern attitudes toward sex—as depicted in works like the highly popular *Kama Sutra*—by the American counterculture of the sixties. The youth of the counterculture practiced "free love," and rock-and-roll played a huge part in its propagation, as evidenced by the anti-establishment battle cry, "sex, drugs, and rock-and-roll."

In terms of a fourth ritual similarity, the use of drugs went hand in hand with the celebration of sex. Despite being more tenuous in terms of details, the similarity regarding the use of drugs is a hallmark of fertility rites and rock-and-roll. While the bacchantes drank wine and/or perhaps chewed a hallucination-producing ivy, the dancers of the early dithyrambs performed under the influence of wine, the sacred drink. The American youth, on the other hand, not only discovered that drugs provided a transrational experience, they openly consumed them as a form of protest. As Arthur Evans asserts in *The God of Ecstasy*, the use of drugs in both the Dionysian tradition and the American counterculture "sharply diverges from patriarchal civilization" because the influence of drugs helps the devotee experience ecstasy and transcend the boundaries of the civilized ego.[16] While sex and the use of drugs were more implicit in the early rock-and-roll cult (perhaps more feared by the public than practiced by the youth), they became explicit in the peace, love, and Rock cult that culminated in the Haight-Ashbury community and at the Woodstock event. "Make love, not war" and "Turn on, Tune in, and Drop Out" clearly express the ritual power of sex and drugs in the hippies' lifestyle.

The fifth ritual similarity concerns the use of words and the respective ways in which they evolved from a non-intellectual, group-possessing and life-affirming factor in the rituals of the bacchae and early rock-and-roll cult to a means for creating a new social awareness. According to Walter Burkert, the "collective scream" offered to Dionysus in the oreibasia, which led the group "to the brink of ecstasy," consisted of the wild shouts, "*euhoi*" and "*thriambe, dithyrambe*."[17] Evans renders the saluatory screams/chants "Euhoi! Euhoi!" as "Hai-ee! Hai-ee!"

and translates "euhios" as "ecstatic."[18] He claims that the "Hai-ee! Hai-ee!" and the "trilled sound of olololo" played a significant role in creating communal ecstasy, invoking the presence of Dionysus and affirming the joy and suffering of life. Because the shouted words served an irrational, if not magical, purpose, the cognitive content had little or no significance. In Burkert's words, this "elementary stratum of invocation is touched by those traditional, linguistically meaningless word-sounds which accompany specific dances or processions" devoted to the ritual fusion with the god.[19]

With a gradual, conscious sophistication of the use of words, the dithyramb became a vehicle for the lower classes' criticism of social injustices imposed by the aristocracy that arose with the creation of the polis. As in the divine mystery initiation rites, the dithyramb consisted of things done, the dromena, and things said, the legomena. The legomena served as a means of interpreting the meaning or power of the dromena's magical ritual acts. The hypokrites, or the exarchon in Ionic, was the actor/interpreter/dithyrambic leader whom the choros danced around and with whom they verbally interacted. While the early performances, as Lillian Lawler states in *The Dance in Ancient Greece*, involved "uncouth gestures, horseplay, and loud, largely extemporized ejaculations in honor of Dionysus, in prose or verse or both," the interaction between the exarchon and choros became more sophisticated in theme and scope.[20] "Without doubt," claims Jack Lindsay in *The Clashing Rocks*, "the process of development in the dithyramb came from the growing tension between the exarchon-hypokrites and the choros."[21] This development converted the ritual forms of the female revolt into a medium of protest.

The distinguishing element of this protest involved a shift from the unconscious to the conscious use of words. The screams and word-chants of the bacchantes were not significant in terms of rational content; rather, these vocalizations were part of the subconscious invocation made during the trance-inducing ritual. The use of words in the original dithyrambs, though imbued with meaning, retained this subconscious function. However, between the changes that Arion introduced in the seventh century B.C. and the 534 performance of Thespis's goat-song (tragoedia), the conscious use of words became an essential part of the drama. According to Lindsay, Herodotus claimed that it was Arion who poeticized the dithyramb by introducing "satyrs speaking in meter."[22] This development—which fueled the anti-aristocratic purposes of the Dionysian cult—turned the spontaneous, unregimented dithyramb into a planned and practiced performance. Thespis established the role of a single actor, the hypokrites, whose interaction with the choros constituted a full-ended performance. As A. W. Pickard-Cambridge argues in *Dithyramb*, "nothing is more likely than that Thespis should have taken in hand a pre-existing extempore speaker, talking to the chorus as he chose to do at the moment, and have made him deliver regularly composed speeches in character."[23] Accompanied by the shift of the unconscious to the conscious use of words, the secularization of the Dionysian impulse changed the essence of the dithyramb from an unconscious mode of expression/worship to an aesthetic means of protesting against repressive social values. This whole process has been summarized by Alan Little in *Myth and Society in Attic Drama*:

> It is for this reason that one should insist on what state recognition meant for tragedy, for the satyr play, and for the Dionysiac dithyramb. It meant change from ritual forms to a new status. It meant the beginning of secularization. When the state took over such embryonic dramatic forms it was in reality converting these forms to its own uses. It was taking over the functions of an earlier society, which had expressed itself in such ritual as a means of maintaining solidarity within the group. It substituted for more primitive conceptions founded in uncritical emotion and expressed in mythological terms a freer means of giving vent to social criticism. Such a transition was, of course, only possible after the political advance had been made from tribal organization and the machinery set up for the actual verbalization of society's needs.[24]

The culmination and the synthesis of the political aims of the state with the religious/social aims of the consolidated lower classes produced a powerful, aesthetic expression of society's needs, spiritual as well as economic, to such a degree that Carl Kerenyi proclaims: "The way in which the Athenian people received and assimilated tragedy and its immanent connection with the dark god is the greatest miracle in all culture history."[25] In sum, whereas the cult of the wild women revolted against social repression in their worship of Dionysus, the lower classes channelled this cultic impulse into a more focused attack against the reigning cultural value system. The state, in turn, secularized the dithyramb of the lower classes, changing the function of the dithyramb from a religious to a secular one, from a glorified drinking bout to an organized public dramatic festival. In the process, this secularization gave birth to drama as a mainstream social event.

Just as the use of words in the oreibasia was aimed at mass possession and not intellectual import, songs of rock-and-roll's first period, from the mid-fifties to mid-sixties, said little to nothing about the impending revolution. It was not the conscious intent of the artist to make an anti-establishment statement in his or her songs. That does not mean that there were not anti-establishment elements in the songs, but they were of the ritual forms and not explicit principles. Artists were singing to free the body, not to inform the intellect. In fact, rock-and-roll artists were often criticized for writing unintelligible, meaningless lyrics, particularly in refrains. While lead singers sang songs about subjects common to the pop field, the other band members joined in on choruses that were often free of any specific intellectual content–such as "sha-la-la," "oh-oh-oh," and "hey, hey." If anything, the majority of early rock-and-roll songs were establishment reaffirming. As Herbert London observes in *Closing the Circle: A Cultural History of the Rock Revolution,* they defended "prosperity, consumerism, contracts, institutional loyalty, power, and reason."[26] Although the songs concerning youth culture affirmed a group identity, this identity was focused on dances, parties, school, fashion, cars, love and courtship, marriage, food, and vacations. Of course, some lyrics suggested unconventional behavior and some artists expressed their loneliness, but early rockers as a group were joyous and impervious to a social role. In fact, their contentment with society and culture is apparent in the respect the songs paid to home, parents, heroes, institutions, the nation's accomplishments, freedom, spending money, television shows and movies, and Christian values. Literally hundreds of songs dealt with the metaphorical concepts of angels, eternal love, heaven, and paradise, as indicated in the following titles: "Earth Angel," "Angel in the Sky," "Teen Angel," "Teenage Heaven," "Ten Commandments of Love," and "Heaven and Paradise." This lyrical tribute to society also included the West's major male-dominated prejudices, particularly against women, who were bluntly regarded as passive objects of beauty, sex, and possession.

Part of the reason for early Rock's society-affirming lyrics was business, which tended to act as a system that filtered out value-threatening texts in an attempt to sell its product. The perfect example is Presley. Under the spell of businessmen, who had highly paid writers in charge of his lyrics, Elvis was careful not to acknowledge black influence of any sort in his songs. Besides racism, a significant reason for the reluctance among aspiring white singers to admit black influence was that the early Rock songs that did contain what society considered revolting lyrics stemmed mostly from the rhythm-and-blues field.

Despite its effort to tame Rock lyrics to assure profit, business felt the weight of the anti-Rock powers, institutional law and public opinion. In 1955, over fifty songs were banned in one week by the Juvenile Delinquency and Crime Commission of Houston, Texas, because of "unacceptable" lyrics. Moreover, juvenile delinquincy was linked to rock-and-roll by a congressional subcommittee. Although Rock lyrics had been "cleansed" by 1956, these forces brought about the payola hearings in 1959 and 1960. Under the assumption that rock-and-roll was bad music and contained immoral lyrics, hearings were conducted by the House of Representatives Special Subcommittee on Legislative Oversight to see if rock-and-roll had been forced upon the American public—that is, if disc jockeys had taken money from record producers, manufacturers, and distributors in return for plugging their product. The end result was, as the authors of Rolling Stone's *Rock of Ages* declare, Rock fell into its "Dark Ages" in the late fifties and early sixties:

> Just as teenagers, with their awesome purchasing power, were being courted by Hollywood and Madison Avenue, rock and roll had passed into the mainstream, fast becoming the province of established cor-

> porate interests rather than the renegade visionaries of the past. For a while, at least, the music would be in the hands of professionals, who knew what teens wanted and how to sell it to them. These developments might have outraged older rockers, who would hardly recognize the fruits of their creative vision. Still, as long as there were teenagers, those teenagers would want a special music that spoke to them. It's just that the language was going to change for a while.[27]

In the early sixties, however, something new was afoot in popular music which would have a revolutionary influence on the lyrics and messages of rock-and-roll artists. The revival of folk music which began in the late fifties with groups like the Kingston Trio was being modified by folk rock's first poets. Although artists like Joan Baez, Phil Ochs, and Peter, Paul, and Mary helped spread the protest-oriented folk music across college campuses, no single figure rises higher in this tradition than Bob Dylan. Armed with a blues harmonica and accompanied by his acoustic guitar, Dylan powerfully aimed his lyrics. Songs like "Blowin' in the Wind" and "The Times They Are A-Changin'" were classic expressions of the revolutionary spirit of the times—a spirit that was captured in the lyrics of Rock artists in the middle to late sixties.

Emboldened by the mass appeal as well as the commercial success of the message-oriented songs of these new folk artists, Rock artists began to attack society's value system and, eventually, to develop a new one. The attack began with, primarily, the Rolling Stones. They negated the core of the Judeo-Christian tradition by embodying its darker side. While their number one hits "(I Can't Get No) Satisfaction" and "Paint It Black" hinted at things to come, their intent became obvious on the 1967 LP, "Their Satanic Majesties Request." Politically, they attempted to destroy the dominant values and to show the fallacy of a separate, better side. In "Sympathy For the Devil" on their 1968 album "Beggar's Banquet," Mick Jagger sings that there is no difference between sinners and saints, that it was society as a whole who killed the Kennedy brothers. On the same record, they belligerently demand a violent revolution (the song "Street Fighting Man" was originally banned in England). Morally, they aimed at a reevaluation of "the good" in relation to instinct, particularly sex. They were joined in this effort by a number of groups, such as the Animals, the Doors, the Jimi Hendrix Experience, Steppenwolf, and Led Zeppelin.

While their manager, Andrew Oldham, helped give the Rolling Stones the image of Rock's original bad boys, the Brian Epstein-guided Beatles assured their ascendency to the top of the music business by creating a clean-despite-their-long-hair, good-boy image. This difference, so prevalent in their lyrics, divided Rock groups into divine- and demonic-oriented ones, a categorization which is still valid. While some of their earlier songs, like "Yesterday" (a lament for the lost innocence of childhood) and "Help," were reminiscent of what made Elvis "lonely," the Beatles accepted their religious role as early as 1965. In his infamous interview with Rolling Stone in 1970, Lennon asserted that after experimenting with LSD, the Beatles "took" the "position" of God or gurus in creating their messages beginning with their hit, "The Word (Is Love)." With their impetus during the counterculture's Summer of Love (1967), Rock's universal love found its highest mystical form.

A very obvious difference in the emphasis of the Beatles' and Stones' lyrics involves Rock's first big issue, sex. For instance, the Beatles sang "I Want to Hold Your Hand" and the Stones sang Willie Dixon's "I Just Want to Make Love to You" on their debut albums. While the Stones incessantly plugged uninhibited sex, the Beatles stuck to the sexual themes of the pop field in their early songs and actually de-emphasized sex in their later songs. While songs like "Wild Thing" and "Take a Walk on the Wild Side" celebrated, a la Stones, the ecstatic aspect of sex, there was a thoughtful side to Rock artists' inquiry into the value of sex. For instance, in "Love in Mind," Neil Young insinuates that religious authorities are to blame for the spiritual devaluation of sex and nature.

While the theme of sex resounds throughout the history of Rock lyrics, it is only a small part of Rock's condemnation of patriarchal values, or, in Roszak's terms, Western technocracy. Roszak reluctantly acknowledges the power of Rock as a medium for creating a new worldview. While he praises the messages of Bob Dylan, questions the relevance of the Beatles' surrealistic songs, and is appalled by the "mock-Dionysian frenzy" of the Doors, Roszak agrees with Timothy Leary that Rock artists are "the real 'prophets' of the rising generation."[28]

In the middle to late sixties, Rock artists developed the following new-paradigm themes: the expansion of consciousness; pantheism, particularly as it relates to the assimilation of Eastern philosophy, universal love, and ecological awareness; and, finally, a return to the primordial state of oneness with the cosmos or nature (which artists related through metaphors such as "home" and "sun").

The expansion of consciousness as a Rock theme accompanied the formation of the counterculture and its assimilation of Eastern thought and psychedelia in the middle to late sixties. Rock artists began to search for a self free not only from the confines of duty and responsibility as practiced and expected by older generations, but also from the established boundaries which distinguished between the race and class (though not the sex) of people. Drugs aided the search. In 1966, on the heels of Ken Kesey and his Merry Pranksters' "acid tests," "acid rock" became a San Francisco phenomenon, ushered in by groups such as the Grateful Dead and Jefferson Airplane. While Dead concerts were purported acid tests in themselves, Jefferson Airplane's 1967 LP, "Surrealistic Pillow," contained the drug song "White Rabbit," which captured the spirit as well as the aims of the drug culture. Building upon Lewis Carroll's fantasy world in *Alice in Wonderland*, "White Rabbit" portrays Alice as an authority on drugs and the dimensions of self which society knows nothing about. Responsible for the death of logic and measurement, the experience from the pills that Alice understands can–unlike any of mother's pills–lead to self-actualization. The song ends with the claim that one should feed one's head. In other words, with the birth of acid rock, the goal of rock-and-roll no longer meant the mere liberation of the body, it insisted on the expansion of consciousness.

By chemically and lyrically exploring a fantasy world beyond social control, Rock artists guided the drug culture's scope, as Van Morrison sings, "Into the Mystic." While other American artists were composing drug/consciousness-raising songs (e.g., Dylan's "Mr. Tambourine Man," the Byrds' "Eight Miles High," and Jimi Hendrix's "Purple Haze"), it was the Beatles, once again, who brought it all home. Their first psychedelic song, "Tomorrow Never Knows," expresses not only the nature, but the *value* of the drug experience: by turning off the conscious mind and merging with mind-at-large, one experiences the self beyond death. While the song contains both Buddhist and Taoist imagery, the fruit of the vision resides in the psyche's knowing embodiment of universal love. The song, in short, espouses pantheism.

Through their Summer-of-Love "concept" albums, "Sergeant Pepper's Lonely Hearts Club Band" and "Magical Mystery Tour," the Beatles helped structure a countercultural value system, lifestyle, and religion. Besides encouraging people to turn on to LSD and to find help through friends and by getting high, they preached on "Sergeant Pepper's" that by "fixing a hole" in one's vision of reality, one allows the mind to wander, which inevitably ensures that things will start "getting better." By taking time for things that were formerly not important, particularly self-actualization, one creates meaning and pur-pose. The theme of pantheism as a replacement for the traditional worldview is most emphatic in "Within You Without You." The song not only reflects the philosophical influence the Beatles' excursion to the Maharashi in India had on them, George Harrison's sitar playing, inspired by Ravi Shankar, gives it a very pervasive Eastern overtone. The text begins with a political accusation that the wall between people has been created by technocrats who have no sense of spiritual truth. The philosophical part of the message is just as clear: by collectively embracing pantheism, people can save the world.

On "Magical Mystery Tour," they reiterate this message in different, yet just as powerful terms. In "I Am the Walrus," John Lennon begins with a cry that humans are all one. This cry serves as an invocation to a communal fusion with Dionysus. Insinuating that life means brutality and suffering, which is why Lennon claims that he is crying, this suffering can be transcended by ecstatically affirming the true self. While he signifies that everyone is a fertility practioner, the walrus is a Dionysian figure whose loud, repetitive, and meaningless refrain confirms the transrational nature of the union. The song-ending chant, which states that everyone has one, signifies universal identity. This identity, as described in "Strawberry Fields Forever," is hard to actualize, but once one has found the way to this utopic, Hindu state of mind, it becomes obvious that nothing in society's world really matters much. The strongest message on the record, anticipated by the first ten songs, sums up the counterculture's highest ideal: "All You Need is Love."

Struck by the Beatles' commercial success and their astounding influence on countercultural sensibilities, other groups quickly followed their lead. For instance, the Moody Blues infused Eastern mysticism, drug overtones, orchestral accompaniments, and technological innovations (particularly in terms of synthesizers and recording equipment) into their sixties' albums. The jacket to their second record, "In Search of the Lost Chord," captures the spirit of their message. Between a large skull and fetus, a yogi with a somber, grey face rises up through a series of faces to a state of enlightenment. The orange and red face at the top, whose six unattached arms are open to the universe, portrays compassion as well as self-actualization. On the jacket's inside, there is a mantra and a brief discussion of the Hindu yantra, OM–which is described as God, Being, and the answer.

What the Moody Blues added to the Beatles' pantheistic message is the role of nature in constituting the new self. Through their poetic translations of Hinduism, however adulterated, they clearly capture the notion of a sacred universe. By listening to "Voices in the Sky," glimpsing "Visions of [a surrealistic] Paradise," and reaching the lost chord, they insist that one discovers that the real "Actor" is nature, a living, thinking being. As indicated by the titles to their fourth and fifth LPs, "To Our Childrens Childrens Children" and "A Question of Balance," the Moody Blues focused their message and echoed the counterculture's cry for peace and a communal-consciousness awakening.

Following the sixties, the call for a new relationship between humankind and nature has remained a Rock theme with two unique slants. The first involves the recognition of the problem, which Dylan stipulates in "All Along the Watchtower": while only society's fools and outcasts recognize that life is no joke, technocrats mindlessly destroy the environment. The second slant is that a new relationship with nature is inevitable. As Spirit implies in "Nature's Way," nature is provoking ecological awareness and action in and of itself by revealing that something is wrong. Or, as the Guess Who proclaim in "No Sugar Tonight/New Mother Nature," the new Mother Nature is taking over.

Rock's pantheistic/environmental theme climaxes in two of its most significant metaphors: "home" and "sun," which refer to the earth, cosmos, and/or the universal self. Both metaphors imply a return to an original state of cosmic unity. While this return for demonic rockers equals the abyss, universal nothingness, or "The End," as Jim Morrison screams in his Oedipal torment, this beginning for divine-oriented groups means the harmonious state of primal being.[29] For instance, in Steely Dan's "Home at Last," Van Morrison's "Into the Mystic," and Peter Gabriel's "Solsbury Hill," home represents a place of blissful cosmic union. This use of home is nowhere clearer or more consistent than in the songs of the Grateful Dead (whose lyricist is Robert Hunter). For instance, in "Ripple," home is the spiritual goal that must be reached alone. It is the source of life, the place beyond man-made invention, where day and night, yin and yang, are one. In "Eyes of the World," the use of home implies that the unity of the individual and the conscious cosmos is made possible by merely waking up to reality. While peace is the aim of returning home in "Brokedown Palace," in "Uncle John's Band," the Dead suggest that–individually or collectively–everyone's return home is inevitable.

Rock's use of "sun" implies the same return. For instance, the Fifth Dimension's "Aquarius/Let the Sunshine In," Donovan's "Sunshine Superman," the Dead's "Here Comes Sunshine," The Doors' "Waiting for the Sun," and the Moody Blues' "Dawning Is The Day" are only a few examples of songs in which the sun signifies a consciousness awakening. The Beatles have a repertoire of songs which does the same. In "Here Comes the Sun" and "The Sun King," the Beatles affirm that the sun will issue in a state of tranquil union. In "It's All Too Much," the sun is a vehicle to an experience of oneness, and in "Across the Universe," the sun is used as a simile for universal love.

Whether associated with the sun, home, the moon, or a garden, the theme of a return to a paradisiacal place resounds throughout Rock lyrics. This theme is one of many that Rock artists have developed, but it shows most clearly the pantheistic vision propagated in the sixties spiritual revolution. In other words, with guidance from rock-and-roll messages, the counterculture which helped establish women's lib, earth day, civil and gay rights, mass anti-war demonstrations, and love-ins flourished in the late 1960s. Although it is impossible to determine to what degree the music influenced the revolutionary thinking and vice-versa, clearly the transformation of rock-and-roll's unconscious revolt into a conscious protest proved a powerful medium in the development as well as the expression of the values of the counterculture.

By virtue of the ability to possess masses of people, Dionysianism and rock-and-roll's cultic rituals involving music, song, dance, and the use of drugs helped spark two of Western civilization's most significant Zeitgeists. As antitheses to established patriarchal orders, each cult's unconscious revolt was transformed into a consciously directed, yet aesthetically expressed protest—a protest which parallels the gradual sophistication of the use of words in their lyrics. In ancient Greece, this sophistication resulted in the birth of drama; in America and Europe in the 1960s, it captured and promoted the worldview of the counterculture.

Conclusion

The Dynamics of Balance as a New-Paradigm Solution to the West's Present Spiritual Crisis

> From this short survey of cultural attitudes and values we can see that our culture has consistently promoted and rewarded the yang, the masculine or self-assertive element of human nature, and has disregarded its yin, the feminine or intuitive aspects. Today, however, we are witnessing the beginning of a tremendous evolutionary movement. The turning point we are about to reach marks, among many other things, a reversal in the fluctuation between yin and yang. As the Chinese text says, "The yang, having reached its climax, retreats in favor of the yin."[1]

Contemporary new-paradigm scholars share the conviction that an impending reintegration of the West's traditionally suppressed feminine, ecological impulse will change the way people feel about their relationships to the environment and to one another. They believe that the present paradigm shift, generated by the sixties Zeitgeist and still being formulated, will enhance the quality of life on earth. Although their sources range from prehistorical times to the present day and their arguments often differ drastically, a common aim unites their theories: to promote the new-paradigm shift. The most consistent formulation of this aim centers on the balance of nature's polarities.

The new-paradigm line of discourse almost always begins with the West's purported spiritual crisis. While eulogizing patriarchal virtues such as reason, control, and progress, the West has sublimated the Archetypal Feminine for over two millenia and thereby forsaken the dynamics of balance exhibited in nature and the human mind. In so doing, the West has generated a law-and-order urge not only to understand nature, but to correct it. This urge—exhibited in the Apollonian principle from ancient Greek philosophy, Christianity, and Roman stoicism to modern science and technology—has cultivated a rational idealism in the West that has suppressed the reverence for nature shared by primal peoples. "Indeed," Alan Watts declares, "the whole enterprise of Western technology is 'to make the world a better place'—to have pleasure without pain, wealth without poverty, and health without sickness.'"[2] It is not the desire for a life of pleasure, wealth, and health that has proven to be so harmful, but the way we have attempted to achieve such a life. Through violent efforts to control naturally complex systems which cannot be broken down into categories of good and evil, the West has confused its wants with its needs, quantity with quality, and facts with value. In effect, we have been blinded by technocratic efficiency. Certain that science has a monopoly on truth, that law is the key to human decency, and that community is constituted by likenesses, we have forced our spiritual needs into a realm beyond legitimate human endeavor.

Although a source of great achievements, the reason-as-virtue paradigm has led Westerners to "regard the universe as different and separate from themselves—that is, as a system of external objects which needs to be subjugated." New-paradigm scholars insist that the danger with this perspective is not only its role in suppressing the means to cultivate identity and harmony with nature, but that it has led people in the technocratic West to tend to act as nature's enemy (to be ego- as opposed to eco-minded). "The point is," Watts concludes, "technology is destructive only in the hands of people who do not realize that they are one and the same process as the universe."[3]

What is needed, new-paradigm scholars concur, is a reintegration of the feminine mystique, the sense of an all-encompassing community of being. In various forms, the processes involved in this reintegration have been the foci in all three periods of the new-paradigm tradition. Whether expressed as reintegrating the unconscious with the ego, reinstituting intuition as a complementary faculty to reason, or re-assessing the values of the technocracy with aims of the counterculture, new-paradigm solutions inevitably involve delineations of the dynamics of balance.

In developing their second line of discourse, the scholars invariably turn to expressions of Earth Wisdom as models of the dynamics of balance. These delineations are drawn often from primal Greek, Indian, and Chinese expressions of nature's interdependent polarities. Recognizing the Mother Goddess, Dionysus, Shiva, and yin as representations of nature's dark, mysterious, female, receptive, synthesizing, and intuitive principles and the Father-sky, Apollo, Vishnu, and yang as light, rational, male, aggressive, and discriminating principles, the scholars contend that only through balancing the two can individuals and society at large actualize full human worth. By juxtaposing Earth Wisdom with the dissolution of balance which was fostered by the West's overemphasis on patriarchal values, the scholars conclude that in order to remedy the West's spiritual crisis, a new balance must be forged. This remedy, in turn, initiates the final step in the new-paradigm discourse: to depict the manifestations of the reintegration of the Dionysus/Shiva/yin impulse in contemporary culture.

Of the innumerable manifestations which scholars have explicated, none are more significant than the movements associated with ecology and feminism. The culminating forces of the countercultural sensibilities and spirituality disseminated by the sixties revolution, ecology and feminism have had the most impact in extending communal-consciousness awareness to include the biosphere. The recovery of the goddess tradition; the deepened appreciation of archaic, esoteric perspectives; and the promulgation of the Gaia hypothesis are but a few examples of ecology's and feminism's spiritual influence. While the Green party is regarded by many scholars as the political manifestation of the spirituality which links feminism and ecology, this spirituality has been expressed also in new-paradigm perspectives concerned with interpreting the findings of the new physics, with reinterpreting the mythology and message of Jesus, and with illuminating the depictions of the new self emerging from psychology.

Using concepts such as chaos, entropy, relativity, complementarity, dissipative structures, and the uncertainty and anthropic principles, new-paradigm scholars—such as Fritjof Capra, Ilya Prigogine, Gary Zukav, and Theodore Roszak—show that in order to transcend the worldview that has dominated the West from the Greek logos to Newtonian mechanics, the belief in notions such as an objective observer and experimental certainty must be replaced by notions of a subjective participant and probabilities, tendencies, and meaningful paradoxes. These changes not only precipitate a new worldview, one in which the whole cannot be split into constituent parts, but they dictate a new approach to understanding reality.

The new worldview supplants the immutable laws of nature, which were once discoverable by analyzing cause-and-effect relationships, with the concept of spontaneous creativity—or, mind-in-nature. From subatomic "particles" to galaxies, the cosmos presents itself as an interconnected, interpenetrating phenomenon which operates as a micro- and macrocosm of interrelated ideas. It is not an object of analyzable absolutes, but a system of interdependent connections which expresses mindfulness. "To see the world as a realm of interrelated ideas," Roszak adduces, "places us in a condition of dialogue; it connects In-here with Out-there as a continuum. It places us on 'speaking terms' with the universe."[4] This condition of dialogue, which presupposes the existence of an evolving cosmic consciousness, binds the human and nonhuman world both physically and spiritually. As such, the link between ecological awareness and the purported worldview of the new physics can be described in terms of a shift in consciousness, one that necessitates the recognition that the universe and everything in it is related in thought.

While the foundation of this view of reality was constructed by quantum theorists early in this century, it was not until after the 1960s revolution that scholars such as Capra started spreading the awareness of the view's spiritual dimensions. One reason that the awareness has spread is that through the counterculture's assimilation of ideas relating to Eastern pantheism, the Mother Goddess, and Gaia, many people have been exposed to and accepted related perspectives.

A similar case exists with another manifestation of the new paradigm, one that is concerned with re-mythologizing Jesus and reinterpreting his message. A century before the dogma-free Jesus freaks of the sixties (not to be confused with the pentacostal Jesus people of the seventies), scholars such as Ralph Waldo Emerson and Friedrich Nietzsche attacked Christian dogma on the basis of its split between spirit and matter. Although the Jesus freaks–one of many intangible groups of the counterculture–did not have a succinct theology, what they had in mind when speaking of Jesus always implied a realized eschatology. An ecumenical symbol representing a state of being or the potential for transformation, the Jesus of the counterculture had, to be sure, only a limited relationship to the reinterpreted Jesus of new-paradigm theologians, but he spoke a similar pantheistic message.

Although the new-paradigm interpretation of the mythology and message of Jesus started with scholars such as Emerson, it was psychologists such as Carl Jung and Erich Neumann who re-mythologized Jesus and reinterpreted his message in terms of an archetypal understanding–namely, that Jesus' crucifixion symbolizes the death of the ego and his resurrection represents the rebirth of the unconscious-integrated ego. This archetypal understanding, which supplanted the concept of the Kingdom in heaven with the Kingdom within, was popularized by–among others–Joseph Campbell. Again, the success of this popularization was in no small part tied to the pantheistic sensibilities cultivated by the counterculture.

Since the middle of the eighties, the notion of Jesus as an archetypal hero who represents the potential for transformation in all humans has been increasingly propounded. Matthew Fox, Thomas Matus, David Steindl-Rast, and Stephen Mitchell are four new-paradigm theologians who have distinguished between the patriarchal, apocalytic teaching *about* Jesus and the pantheistic, eros-oriented teaching *of* Jesus. Together, the work of these scholars supplies an amalgamation of new-paradigm perspectives on issues regarding the message and mythology of the newly-crowned, ecofeminist Christ.

In *The Coming of the Cosmic Christ*, Mathew Fox enumerates the theological paradigm shift as moving from anthropocentrism to a living cosmology, from rational thought to mystical experience, from obedience-as-virtue to creativity-as-virtue, from sense-suppressing dogma to erotic worship, and from theism to pantheism. He explains that the shift is occurring in two significant ways: the quest for the historical Jesus has become the quest for the Cosmic Christ and the concept of a realized eschatology has replaced the belief in a futuristic eschatology. In order to free the universality of Jesus and his message from the age-old, patriarchal-dominated kerygma and myth, he contends that it is necessary to recognize that the Cosmic Christ represents an evolving, communal experience of the mystical cosmos and to understand that the "kingdom/queendom" which Jesus taught was within, here and now, rather than a Kingdom in heaven or a future world which was prophesied to begin on Judgment Day. By reinterpreting the crucifixion story in terms of the patriarchal crucifixion of Mother Earth and the resurrection story as the rebirth of a living cosmology based on Mother Earth, Fox attempts to revitalize the Christian faith, making it more ecumenical, feminine-integrated, and experiential. While exposing weaknesses in the religion's traditionally narrow, androcentric, redeemer-redeemed theology, he transports salvation out of the realm of the personal and anchors it in a process of communal healing through compassion.

As does Fox, Thomas Matus and David Steindl-Rast regard the theological new paradigm as holistic and ecumenical and the old one as rationalistic, bound to scholastic, proof-oriented interpretations. In *Belonging to the Universe*, Matus and Steindl-Rast describe five criteria for theological new-paradigm thinking, criteria which parallel Fritjof Capra's delineation of new-paradigm thinking in science. Their first two criteria deal with God's revelation. In place of a static set of revealed truths captured in dogma, new-paradigm theology approaches God's revelation as a dynamic process of self-manifestation. Hence, dogma is relegated to the realm of particular, static moments of God's self-manifestation, whereas salvation—regarded as a future event in the old paradigm—becomes the ever-present, dynamic truth of this self-manifestation.

The experiential aspects of revelation and salvation dictate, according to Matus and Steindl-Rast, changes in the methods and approaches of theologians attempting to interpret Christian kerygma and myth. By synthesizing these changes into three criteria, the scholars explain, first, why theology must be regarded as a process of knowing—including the affective, intuitive, and mystical realm—instead of an objective science. Second, theological statements do not build a monolithic system of laws and doctrine but create a network of perspectives relative to an authentic faith. Third, there is no compendium or "summa" of theological knowledge because doctrine offers only a limited expression of the experiential truth it attempts to convey.

While these criteria have drastic implications for the reinterpretation of Jesus and his teachings, the central implication is that the preaching about Jesus relates to a confined historical context while the teaching of Jesus relates to a universal religious understanding. As Steindl-Rast explains:

> We must always refer back to the teaching *of* Jesus himself. Jesus had a deep mystic experience of God and spoke about it, lived it, in terms of the Kingdom of God. "Kingdom of God" meant for Jesus "the saving power of God made manifest in human history." For Jews at the time of Jesus, salvation was a matter of the community to which they belonged. For us this communal aspect of salvation is almost impossible to appreciate except in terms of global community.[5]

In *The Gospel According to Jesus*, Stephen Mitchell adopts Matus's and Steindl-Rast's methodological criteria to distinguish between the two depictions of Jesus and to formulate a consistent translation of Jesus' authentic teachings. Convinced that the New Testament scholarship of the past seventy-five years has done much to free Jesus' authentic teachings, Mitchell admits that his methodology is based more on "a mode of listening" than a proof-text, analytic interpretation. He separates the authentic Jesus from the "later Jesus," whose teaching had been adulterated by the apocalyptic fervor which accompanied the belief in the soon-to-come Kingdom of heaven. The differences between the two figures are obvious, as Mitchell clearly delineates:

> Jesus teaches us, in his sayings and by his actions, not to judge (in the sense of not to condemn), but to keep our hearts open to all people;

> the later "Jesus" is the archetypal judge, who will float down terribly on the clouds for the world's final rewards and condemnations. Jesus cautions against anger and teaches the love of enemies; "Jesus" calls his enemies "children of the Devil" and attacks them with the utmost vituperation and contempt. Jesus talks of God as a loving father, even to the wicked; "Jesus" preaches a god who will cast the disobedient into everlasting flames. Jesus includes all people when he calls God "your Father in heaven"; "Jesus" says "*my* Father in heaven." Jesus teaches that all those who make peace, and all those who love their enemies, are sons of God; "Jesus" refers to himself as "*the* Son of God."[6]

The upshot of Mitchell's delineation is that in order for Christianity to regain its relevence, Jesus' message must be interpreted in a universal, pantheistic vein. Hence, the religion's dogma, kerygma, and myth must relinquish their patriarchal, apocalyptically wrought Kingdom in heaven for Jesus' authentic teaching of the Kingdom of God as "a state of being." In other words, the new-paradigm conception of Christ necessitates the assimilation of an ecofeminist position in the processes of interpreting both the mythology surrounding him and the teachings attributed to him.

Obviously, psychology has helped establish the characteristics of the new-paradigm, ecofeminist Christ. Jung, Neumann, and Campbell, for instance, have not only reinterpreted the mythology of Jesus in an archetypal framework, they have helped constitute the meaning of the universal heroic transformation in general. This archetypal transformation has helped create a new-paradigm vision of a balanced self, a self which harmonizes the powers of intuition with the intellect and those of the ego with the unconscious. The theoretical construction of this self has been the primary goal of new-paradigm scholarship.

The new-paradigm self incorporates the erotic or ecstatic aspects of the psyche with the virtues of moderation and discipline, complements work with play, and balances the urge for control with the need for spontaneity. A balanced person maintains an equilibrium between, in Freudian terms, the id and the super-ego or, in Nietzschean terms, the Dionysian and the Apollonian. This individual is both trusting and skeptical, emotional and stoic, consolidating and cooperative as well as competitive and aggressive. By embodying nature's *coincidentia oppositorum*, the balanced person learns to flow between the inner and outer worlds, to harmonize the mystical and rational, and to connect his or her sense of the self with nature.

From the theories of Nietzsche and Emerson to the founding of ecopsychology, the proclamation of the need to reintegrate the identification of self with nature has proliferated. To overcome the profound gulf between nature and humankind that the ego-centered, reason-dominated collective psyche of Western civilization has cultivated, we need to reconsider the traditionally sustained dichotomies such as spirit and matter, mind and body, and the sacred and profane. Absolute dichotomies do not exist in nature or the self. A rekindling of the connection between the self and nature is imperative, for only then can the recognition of the unity of all living creatures be put into practice. The result would not only encourage an amelioration in the relationships between human societies, it would re-connect humankind with the natural environment.

It is precisely the lack of such a connection which accounts for the West's present spiritual crisis, a crisis indicative of the configuration of the postmodern mind. The pluralism, disassociation, uncertainty, and fragmentation which have accompanied the breaking down of the old patriarchal paradigm—including its absolute worldview and value system—have left a void; but they have created also the potential for tranformation. If new-paradigm scholars are right, the transformation has begun. One of the clearest signs that a resolution is in sight centers on the rising awareness of the value of feminine virtues. In various forms, the Western psyche is in the process of reintegrating—both consciously and unconsciously—the principles of mystery, imagination, instinct, cooperation, emotion, and sensitivity in both men and women. To fully achieve such a reintegration, the masculine principles which have characterized the rise and development of Western civilization must be sacrificed in what new-paradigm psychologists call an immense "ego death." By surrendering some of the ego's power to control, dominate, and possess, the emergence of a unified masculine and feminine self is made possible. Solely through a healing reunion of both principles, a reunion in which all opposites are actualized, can individuals and society at large inculcate the lost female essence of being human. Only then can the disconnected, spiritually destitute postmodern mind be transformed into an informed and resolute contemporary mind.

New-paradigm scholars have systematized this transformation. They have helped articulate a new vision of reality, called for a new lifestyle based on countercultural sensibilities, revitalized religious eroticism, and simultaneously cultivated the awareness of the value of a balanced self. While spreading the realization that the millenia-long patriarchal suppression of the feminine, instinctual, and intuitive aspects of the self must be remedied, the scholars have shown that not only is the achievement of full human worth at stake, but the very survival of our species may rest in the balance. As such, new-paradigm scholarship is itself a manifestation of the contemporary mind. It has not only reported the inevitability of a cultural transformation, it has participated in the processes involved in the reintegration of the ecological, feminine impulse, a reintegration based on a reverence for the dynamics of balance apparent in nature and at work in the human mind.

Notes

For full publication information of these citations, see Bibliography.

Preface

1. Tarnas, *Passion*, p. 402.
2. Ibid., p. 422.
3. Ibid., p. 405.
4. Ibid., p. 408.

Introduction

1. Wilber, *Eye To Eye*, p. 1.
2. Kuhn, *Scientific Revolutions*, p. viii.
3. Devall, *Deep Ecology*, p. 144.
4. Watts, *Tao*, pp. 20-21.
5. Ferguson, *Aquarian Conspiracy*, p. 21.
6. Capra, *Belonging*, pp. 179-180.

Introduction to Part One

1. Devall, *Deep Ecology*, p. ix.
2. Roszak, *Counter Culture*, p. xi.
3. Jung, *Undiscovered Self*, p. 121.
4. See Nietzsche, *Der Antichrist*, p. 167; Watts, *Tao*, p. xvi; Jung, *Psychological Types*, p. xi; Keen, *Apology*, p. 17; Neumann, *Origins*, p. xxiv; Campbell, *Masks: Oriental*, p. xii; Roszak, *Counter Culture*, p. 9; Eliade, *Eternal Return*, pp. xi-xii; Capra, *Turning Point*, p. 17.
5. *Emerson*, ed. Spiller, pp. 200 and 179-180.
6. See Marcuse, "Auch dies war eine Stimme Amerikas," p. 4.
7. Neumann, *Great Mother*, p. 336.
8. Neumann, "Mystical Man," *Eranos*, vol. 3, p. 377. The term "man" as used by Neumann is reflective of the sexist language which typifies Western culture. Throughout this book, the term "man" is cited in quotations from a number of eminent scholars. In most other cases, for the lack of a better term, I will use "humankind."

Chapter One

1. *Emerson*, ed. Whicher, pp. 195-196.
2. See Nietzsche, *Nachgelassenes Fragmente*, pp. 660-662.
3. *Emerson*, ed. Spiller, p. 265.
4. Ibid., p. 277.
5. Ibid., pp. 215-216.
6. *Emerson*, ed. Whicher, pp. 105-106.
7. Ibid., p. 51.
8. For a detailed discussion, see Thurin, *Emerson as Priest of Pan* and Yoder, *Emerson and the Orphic Poet in America*.
9. Emerson, *Complete Writings*, pp. 339-353.
10. See Detweiler, "The Over-Rated 'Over-Soul'," pp. 307-309.
11. For a detailed discussion, see *Emerson's Relevance Today*.
12. Waggoner, ed., *Hawthorne*, p. v.
13. Segal, *Joseph Campbell*, p. 101.
14. Quoted in de Angulo, "Comments on a Doctoral Thesis," *C. G. Jung Speaking*, p. 208; Neumann, *Origins*, p. 266.
15. Neumann, *Great Mother*, pp. 57, 25, and 54n.

Chapter Two

1. Eliade, *Eranos*, vol. 4, p. xviii.
2. Froebe-Kapteyn, *Eranos*, vol. 2, p. xvi.
3. *Eranos*, vols. 1-6, Appendices.
4. Jung, *Eranos*, vol. 5, p. xi.
5. *Eranos*, vols. 1-6, Appendices.
6. Jung, *Analytical Psychology*, p. 133.
7. Jung, *Psychological Types*, pp. 215-217.
8. Jung, *Psychological Reflections*, p. 259.
9. Campbell, *Eranos*, vol. 1, p. xii.
10. Jung, *Psychology and Religion*, p. 468.
11. Eliade, *Eranos*, vol. 4, p. xix.
12. Eliade, *Patterns*, pp. xiv-xv and 419. On page xv of *The Myth of the Eternal Return*, Eliade states that he uses the term "archetype" to mean an "exemplary model," not as a structure of the collective unconscious.
13. Eliade, *Patterns*, p. 420.
14. Ibid., p. 456.
15. Eliade, *Eternal Return*, p. 162.
16. Eliade, *Two and One*, pp. 10-11.
17. Campbell, *Eranos*, vol. 4, p. xvi.
18. Campbell, *Hero*, p. 20.
19. Campbell, *Mythic Image*, p. 62.
20. Campbell, *Masks: Occidental*, p. 21.
21. Campbell, *Eranos*, vol. 6, p. xi.
22. Campbell, *Hero*, p. 4.
23. Jung, *Jung Speaking*, pp. 229-230.
24. Eliade, *Eranos*, vol. 4, p. xxi.

Chapter Three

1. Capra, *Turning Point*, p. 45.
2. Anderson, *Upstart Spring*, p. 1.
3. See Anderson, *Upstart Spring*, p. 12.
4. Watts, *Joyous Cosmology*, pp. xiii-xiv.
5. Anderson, *Upstart Spring*, p. 5.
6. *The Esalen Catalog*, January-June, 1993.
7. Needleman, ed., *Sacred Tradition*, pp. vii and 1-2.
8. Watts, *In My Own Way*, p. 297.
9. Capra, *Wisdom*, pp. 26 and 118.
10. Eisler, *The Chalice*, p. 169.
11. See Capra's *Turning Point* and *Wisdom*; Roszak's *Counter Culture* and *Person/Planet*; and Keen's *Voices* and *Fire.*
12. Keen, *Voices*, pp. 155 and 16.
13. See Anderson, *Upstart Spring*, pp. 263-264.
14. Roszak, *Counter Culture*, p. 133.
15. Roszak, *Wasteland*, p. 100.
16. Roszak, *Unfinished Animal*, pp. 171 and 197-203.
17. Roszak, *Person/Planet*, pp. 195-196.
18. Keen, *Dancing God*, p. xxii.
19. Capra, *Wisdom*, pp. 13-14.

Introduction to Part Two

1. Campbell, *Masks: Oriental*, p. 516.
2. Jung, *Memories*, p. 103.
3. Tarnas, *Passion*, p. 444.
4. Capra, *Turning Point*, p. 16.

Chapter Four

1. Nietzsche, *Will*, p. 54.
2. Nietzsche, *Beyond Good*, p. 115.
3. Ibid., pp. 162-163.
4. Roszak, "Friedrich Nietzsche/Woman De-Feminized," *Masculine/ Feminine*, p. 3.
5. Friedrich, "Aristophanes, Nietzsche, and the Death of Tragedy," p. 6.
6. Derrida, *Writing and Difference*, p. 292.
7. Norris, *Deconstruction*, p. 57.
8. Wilamowitz-Moellendorf, *Greek Historical Writing*, p. 32.
9. Nietzsche, *Self-Criticism*, p. 19.
10. Nietzsche, *Birth*, p. 47.
11. Ibid., pp. 47, 73, and 130.
12. Campbell, *Masks: Occidental*, p. 141.
13. Nietzsche, *Birth*, p. 33.

14. Ibid., p. 95.
15. Ibid., pp. 80 and 50.
16. Nietzsche, *Will*, p. 242.
17. Ibid., p. 543.
18. Nietzsche, *Beyond Good*, p. 139.
19. Nietzsche, *Will*, p. 531.
20. See Nietzsche, *Will*, p. 460.
21. Bachofen, *Mother Right*, p. 587.
22. See Otto, *Dionysus*.
23. Nietzsche, *Will*, p. 539.

Chapter Five

1. Neumann, *Great Mother*, p. 336.
2. See Neumann, *Origins*, p. 261ff.
3. Neumann, *Great Mother*, p. 18.
4. Neumann, *Origins*, pp. xiv, 13, and 11.
5. Ibid., p. 126.
6. Neumann, *Origins*, p. 131.
7. Neumann, "Mystical Man," *Eranos*, vol. 6, p. 390.
8. Neumann, *Origins*, pp. 219, 221, 256, xxiv, and 393.
9. Neumann, *Great Mother*, pp. vi and xiii.
10. Ibid., p. 45.
11. Neumann, "Mystical Man," *Eranos*, vol. 6, p. 336.

Chapter Six

1. Watts, *Psychotherapy*, p. 58.
2. Watts, *Tao*, p. 21.
3. Watts, *Nature*, p. 143.
4. Watts, *Two Hands*, pp. 19, 41, and 40.
5. Watts, *Nature*, p. 89.
6. Ibid., p. 41.
7. Watts, *Two Hands*, p. 34.
8. Watts, *Beyond Theology*, pp. 61-62.
9. Watts, *Tao*, p. 20.
10. Watts, *Nature*, pp. 62-63.
11. Ibid., pp. 4 and 60.
12. Ibid., pp. 6 and 9.
13. Watts, *Tao*, pp. 19-20.
14. Ibid., p. 44.
15. Ibid., p. 118.
16. Watts, *Nature*, p. 112.
17. Ibid., pp. 95-96.
18. Watts, *Tao*, p. 54.
19. Watts, *Nature*, p. 119.

Chapter Seven

1. Roszak, "Beyond the Reality Principle," p. 61.
2. Roszak, *Counter Culture*, p. 55.
3. Ibid., p. 240.
4. Ibid., p. 265.
5. Roszak, *Person/Planet*, pp. xxiii, xxv, and xix.
6. Ibid., pp. 45, 47, and 43.
7. Roszak, *The Voice*, pp. 55 and 14.
8. Ibid., pp. 126 and 213.
9. Ibid., p. 320.
10. Ibid., p. 289.
11. Ibid., pp. 304-305.
12. Roszak, *Person/Planet*, p. xxi.

Chapter Eight

1. Capra, *Tao*, p. 307.
2. Ibid., p. 185.
3. See *Albert Einstein: Philosopher-Scientist*, ed., P. A. Schilpp, p. 45.
4. Capra, *Belonging*, p. 70.
5. Capra, *Tao*, pp. 324-328.
6. Ibid., p. 341.
7. Capra, *Turning Point*, pp. 42-43.
8. Ibid., pp. 43-44. Koestler's notion of holons is developed in his book *Janus*.
9. See Wilber, *The Spectrum of Consciousness*.
10. Capra, *Wisdom*, p. 124.
11. Ibid., p. 125.
12. Ibid., p. 14.
13. Capra and Spretnak, *Green Politics*, pp. xix-xx.

Chapter Nine

1. Keen, *Passionate Life*, p. 236.
2. Keen, *Dancing God*, p. ix.
3. Keen, *Apology*, p. 63.
4. Ibid., p. 90.
5. Ibid., pp. 158-159.
6. Ibid., pp. 203 and 198.
7. Keen, *Life Maps*, pp. 103-105.
8. Ibid., p. 109.
9. Ibid., pp. 124-125.
10. Ibid., p. 126.
11. Keen, *Passionate Life*, p. 27.
12. Ibid., pp. 4-5.
13. Ibid., p. 51.

14. Ibid., p. 156.
15. Ibid., p. 5.
16. Ibid., p. 231.
17. Keen, *Fire*, p. 7.
18. Ibid., p. 79.
19. Ibid., p. 153.
20. Keen, *Passionate Life*, pp. 126-127.

Chapter Ten

1. Eisler, "The Goddess of Nature," p. 4.
2. Eisler, *Chalice*, pp. xi-xiiv and xv.
3. Ibid., p. 105.
4. Gimbutas, "The First Wave," p. 281.
5. Eisler, *Chalice*, pp. xvii and xx.
6. Ibid., p. 59.
7. Ibid., p. xv.
8. Ibid., p. 120.
9. Ibid., pp. 169 and 144-145.

Introduction to Part Three

1. Reich, *The Greening*, pp. 2-3.
2. Ibid., p. 4.
3. Asante, *Afrocentricity*, p. 7.
4. Ibid., pp. 94-95.
5. Roszak, *Counter Culture*, p. 1.
6. Reich, *The Greening*, p. 2.
7. Capra, *Turning Point*, p. 415.
8. Roszak, *Person/Planet*, p. 45.
9. Sessions, "Deep Ecology versus Ecofeminism," p. 91.
10. Naess quoted in *Deep Ecology*, p. 74. See Stephen Bodian, "Simple in Means, Rich in Ends: A Conversation with Arne Naess," *Ten Directions* (Summer/Fall 1982).

Chapter Eleven

1. Kerouac, *Dharma*, pp. 202-203.
2. See Louria, *The Drug Scene*.
3. Pirsig, *Zen*, p. 49.
4. Scheler, *Sympathy*, pp. 110, 125, 84, 105, and 127.
5. Pirsig, *Zen*, p. xiii.
6. Roszak, *Counter Culture*, pp. 135-136. See Alan Watts, "Beat Zen, Square Zen, and Zen," *This Is It*.
7. Everson, "Dionysus and the Beat Generation," p. 181.
8. Roszak, *Counter Culture*, pp. 136-137.
9. Kerouac, *Dharma*, pp. 32 and 39.

10. Ibid., p 30. Ryder's "favorite doll"–whom he possibly even loves–is Psyche (the name of Eros's lover in Apuleius's famous tale).
11. Roszak, *Counter Culture*, p. 136.
12. Scheler, *Sympathy*, p. 125.
13. Hipkiss, *Kerouac*, p. 70.
14. Kerouac, *Dharma*, p. 240.
15. Ibid., p. 114.
16. Roszak, *Counter Culture*, p. 145.
17. Hipkiss, *Kerouac*, p. 70.
18. Ibid., p. 70.
19. Kerouac, *Dharma*, p. 141.
20. Ibid., pp. 64-65.
21. Nygren, *Agape and Eros*, p. 210.
22. Kerouac, *Dharma*, pp. 5 and 84.
23. Hipkiss, *Kerouac*, p. 134.
24. Pirsig, *Zen*, p. 135. In his edification of eros, Pirsig indirectly, yet completely excludes agape. That is, in *Zen*, there is no sense in which love involves a reaching down from a transcendent God; rather, Pirsig's development of love is based strictly on the awareness and cultivation of the inner daemon.
25. Sheppard, "The Enormous Vroom," p. 99. In Plato's *Phaedrus*, Socrates explains to Phaedrus that eros is divine madness which transcends visible, physical beauty and is able to bring forth the beauty and truth of one's soul.
26. Pirsig, *Zen*, p. 4.
27. Regarding the superficiality in Pirsig's philosophy, in his article, "Praise God, From Whom All Ball Bearings Flow" (p. 94), Richard Todd argues that there is a "certain ominous hollowness to his arguments" and that Pirsig attempts "to render more than he fully understands."
28. Pirsig, *Zen*, pp. 272, 253, and 293.
29. Kitto, *The Greeks*, p. 58.
30. Pirsig, *Zen*, pp. 340, 280, and 324.
31. Ibid., p. 323.
32. Ibid., p. 315.
33. Northrop, *The Meeting*, p. 54.
34. Pirsig, *Zen*, pp. 106 and 200.
35. Ibid., pp. 230 and xxi.

Chapter Twelve

1. Pattison, *The Triumph of Vulgarity*, p. 40.
2. Although rock-and-roll owes its origins in part to Europe, particularly England, its development as a medium for mass revolt and protest was, as Richard Aquila (*That Old Time Rock and Roll*, p. 23) insists, "99.9 percent American." That is, unlike in England, where the youth of the lower classes identified with rock-and-roll, the middle class youth of America, with leisure time and purchasing power, turned it into a cult–albeit a commercialized one.

3. The reason I differentiate between commercially successful and mass-appreciated songs is because with the growing success of LP sales, many Rock songs that had not made it to the charts had and still have mass impact. Also, the longer version of commercially successful songs, such as the Doors' hit *Light My Fire* helped initiate FM programming which instantly enhanced the chances of a non-hit becoming mass appreciated.
4. Plato, *Dialogues*, ed. Hamilton, p. 1294 (*Laws* 3.700d-e).
5. Ibid., p. 1266 (*Laws* 2.669e-670a).
6. In business terms, Rock was and is "pop" or popular music; however, it is categorically different from the "pop" style of music (a la Perry Como, Andy Williams, and Frank Sinatra) that existed at its inception and still thrives commercially. To add to this ambiguity, Rock music is "pop" also in terms of "pop culture."
7. When asked why he thought rock-and-roll meant so much to people, John Lennon said: "because the best stuff is primitive enough and has no bullshit. It gets through to you, it's beat, go to the jungle and they have the rhythm. It goes throughout the world and it's as simple as that, you get the rhythm going because everybody goes into it. I read that Eldridge Cleaver said that Blacks gave the middle class whites back their bodies, and put their minds and bodies together. It's something like that . . ." (Wenner, *Lennon Remembers*, p. 116).

   Also, as Herbert London argues in *Closing the Circle* (p. 16), "the story of rock is ostensibly the imprint of black music on white America, with all that it suggests. The musical roots go back to Africa, but the lyrical origins are related to the black experience with oppression in this land."
8. Fats Domino quoted in Marc Eliot's *Rockonomics*, p. vi.
9. Orman, *Rock Music*, p. 4.
10. Pattison, *Triumph*, p. 185.
11. It is obviously indeterminable as to what sexual activities the bacchantes practiced; however, as Burkert claims in *Homo Necans* (p. 58): "If the themes of killing and eating are so intensely enacted in ritual that they are able to grip, move, and transform human personality, it is inconceivable that the most powerful human impulse, sexuality, would play no part. On the contrary, sexuality is always intimately involved in ritual." It is also worth noting that the famous incident of 186 B.C. which led to the bacchantes being tried before the Senate had sexual implications. The case concerned the bacchantes' wish to engage in sexual activities with a young man for ritual purposes.
12. See Lindsay, *Clashing Rocks*, p. 329.
13. Nuttall, *Bomb Culture*, pp. 23-24.
14. See Martin, *Anti-Rock*, pp. 60-61.
15. Melly, *Revolt*, p. 40.
16. Evans, *Ecstasy*, p. 184.
17. Burkert, *Greek Religion*, p. 74.
18. Evans, *Ecstasy*, p. 56.
19. Burkert, *Greek Religion*, p. 74.
20. Lawler, *Dance*, p. 5.
21. Lindsay, *Clashing Rocks*, pp. 334-335.

22. Ibid., p. 61.
23. Pickard-Cambridge, *Dithyramb*, pp. 86-87.
24. Little, *Myth and Society*, p. 9.
25. Kerenyi, *Dionysos*, p. 331.
26. London, *Closing the Circle*, p. 36.
27. Ward, *Rock of Ages*, p. 224.
28. Roszak, *Counter Culture*, pp. 1 and 291.
29. At the end of the song, Morrison screams that he wants to kill his Father and have sex with his Mother.

Conclusion

1. Capra, *Turning Point*, p. 45.
2. Watts, *Tao*, p. 20.
3. Ibid., p. 21.
4. Roszak, *The Voice*, p. 172.
5. Steindl-Rast, *Belonging*, p. 57.
6. Mitchell, *The Gospel*, p. 8.

Bibliography

Aquila, Richard. *That Old Time Rock and Roll: A Chronicle of an Era, 1954-1963*. New York: Schirmer Books, 1989.

Anderson, Walter. *The Upstart Spring: Esalen and the American Awakening*. Reading, Mass.: Addison-Wesley, 1983.

Asante, Molefi. *Afrocentricity*. Trenton: Africa World Press, 1988.

Bachofen, J. J. *Myth, Religion, and Mother Rite*. tr. Ralph Manheim. Princeton: Princeton University Press, 1967.

Burkert, Walter. *Greek Religion*. Cambridge: Harvard University Press, 1985.

——. *Homo Necans: The Anthropology of Ancient Greek Sacrificial Ritual and Myth*. Berkeley: University of California Press, 1983.

Campbell, Joseph. *The Masks of God*, 4 vols. New York: Penguin Books, 1976.

——. *The Hero with a Thousand Faces*. Princeton: Princeton University Press, 1973.

——. *The Mythic Image*. Princeton: Princeton University Press, 1981.

——, ed. *Papers from the Eranos Yearbooks*, 6 vols. New York: Bollingen Foundation, 1954-1968.

Capra, Fritjof. *The Tao of Physics*. New York: Bantam Books, 1983.

——. *The Turning Point*. Boston: New Science Library, 1985.

——. *Uncommon Wisdom: Conversations with Remarkable People*. New York: Bantam Books, 1988.

——, David Steindl-Rast, and Thomas Matus. *Belonging to the Universe*. San Francisco: Harper Collins, 1992.

—— and Charlene Spretnak. *Green Politics*. New York: E. P. Dutton, 1984.

de Angulo, Ximina. "Comments on a Doctoral Thesis," *C. G. Jung Speaking*, eds. William McGuire and R. F. C. Hull. Princeton: Princeton University Press, 1977, pp. 206-212.

Derrida, Jacques. *Writing and Difference*. tr. Alan Bass. London: Routledge and Keegan Paul, 1978.

Detweiler, Robert. "The Over-Rated 'Over-Soul'." *Critical Essays on R. W. Emerson*. eds. Robert Burkholder and Joel Myerson. Boston: G. K. Hall, 1983, pp. 307-309.

Devall, Bill and George Sessions. *Deep Ecology*. Salt Lake City: Gibbs M. Smith, 1985.

Eisler, Riane. *The Chalice and the Blade: Our History, Our Future*. San Francisco: Harper & Row, 1988.

——. "The Goddess of Nature and Spirituality: An Ecomanifesto." *In All Her Names*. eds. Joseph Campbell and Charles Muses. New York: Harper Collins, 1991, pp. 3-23.

Eliade, Mircea. *Myth and Reality*. New York: Harper Torchbook, 1963.

——. *The Myth of the Eternal Return, or, Cosmos and History*. Princeton: Princeton University Press, 1971.

——. *Patterns in Comparative Religion*. New York: New American Library, 1974.

——. *The Two and the One*. London: Harville Press, 1965.

Eliot, Marc. *Rockonomics*. New York: Franklin Watts, 1989.

Emerson, Ralph Waldo. *Selected Essays, Lectures, and Poems.* ed. R. E. Spiller. New York: Washington Square Press, 1965.

——. *The Complete Writings.* New York: Wm. H. Wise, 1929.

——. *Selections from Ralph Waldo Emerson.* ed. Stephen Whicher. Boston: Houghton Mifflin, 1957.

Emerson's Relevance Today: A Symposium. Hartford: Transcendental Books, 1971.

Evans, Arthur. *The God of Ecstasy: Sex Roles and the Madness of Dionysos.* New York: St. Martin's Press, 1988.

Everson, William. "Dionysus and the Beat Generation." *The Beats: Essays in Criticism.* ed. Lee Bartlett. London: McFarland, 1981, pp. 181-194.

Ferguson, Marilyn. *Aquarian Conspiracy.* New York: St. Martin's Press, 1980.

Fox, Matthew. *The Coming of the Cosmic Christ.* San Francisco: Harper and Row, 1988.

Friedrich, Rainer. "Aristophanes, Nietzsche, and the Death of Tragedy." *Dionysius,* vol. 4 (December 1980), pp. 5-36.

Gimbutas, Marija. "The First Wave of Eurasian Steppe Pastoralists into Copper Age Europe." *Journal of Indo-European Studies* 5 (Winter 1977), pp. 280-294.

Hipkiss, Robert. *Jack Kerouac: Prophet of the New Romanticism.* Lawrence: The Regents Press of Kansas, 1976.

Jung, C. G. *The Collected Works,* 8 vols. eds. Herbert Read, Michael Fordham, and Gerhard Adler. Princeton: Princeton University Press, 1928.

——. *Analytical Psychology: Its Theory and Practice.* New York: Vintage Books, 1968.

——. *The Undiscovered Self.* New York: New American Library, 1957.

——. *The Essential Jung*. ed. Anthony Storr. Princeton: Princeton University Press, 1983.

——. *Memories, Dreams, Reflections*. ed. Aniela Jaffe. New York: Vintage Books, 1965.

——. *C. G. Jung Speaking: Interviews and Encounters*. eds. William McGuire and R. F. C. Hull. Princeton: Princeton University Press, 1977.

Keen, Sam (in discussion with Jim Fowler). *Life Maps*. ed. Jerome Berryman. Minneapolis: Winston Press, 1978.

——. *The Passionate Life: Stages of Loving*. New York: Harper and Row, 1983.

——. *Fire in the Belly: On Being a Man*. New York: Bantam Books, 1991.

——. *To a Dancing God*. San Francisco: Harper, 1970.

——. *Apology for Wonder*. New York: Harper and Row, 1969.

——, ed. *Voices and Visions*. New York: Harper and Row, 1976.

Kerenyi, Carl. *Dionysos*. Princeton: Princeton University Press, 1976.

Kerouac, Jack. *Dharma Bums*. New York: Penguin Books, 1958.

Kitto, H. D. F. *The Greeks*. New York: Penguin Books, 1957.

Koestler, Arthur. *Janus*. London: Hutchinson Press, 1978.

Kuhn, Thomas. *The Structure of Scientific Revolutions*. Chicago: Chicago University Press, 1970.

Lawler, Lillian. *The Dance in Ancient Greece*. Middletown, Ct.: Wesleyan University Press, 1965.

Lindsay, Jack. *The Clashing Rocks: A Study of Early Greek Religion and Culture and the Origins of Drama.* London: Chapman and Hall, 1965.

Little, Alan. *Myth and Society in Attic Drama.* New York: Octagon Books, Inc., 1967.

London, Herbert. *Closing the Circle: A Cultural History of the Rock Revolution.* Chicago: Nelson-Hall, 1984.

Louria, Donald. *The Drug Scene.* New York: McGraw-Hill, 1968.

Lovelock, J. E. *Gaia, a New Look at Life on Earth.* Oxford: Oxford University Press, 1979.

Marcuse, Ludwig. "Auch dies war eine Stimme Amerikas." *Die Zeit*, Hamburg (April 25, 1957), pp. 4-5.

Martin, Linda and Kerry Segrave. *Anti-Rock: the Opposition to Rock and Roll.* Hamden, Ct.: Archon Books, 1988.

Melly, George. *Revolt into Style.* New York: Anchor Books, 1971.

Mitchell, Stephen. *The Gospel According to Jesus.* New York: Harper Collins, 1993.

Needleman, Jacob and Dennis Lewis, eds. *Sacred Tradition and Present Need.* New York: Viking Press, 1975.

Neumann, Erich. *The Origins and History of Consciousness.* Princeton: Princeton University Press, 1954.

——. *The Great Mother: An Analysis of the Archetype.* Princeton: Princeton University Press, 1963.

——. "Mystical Man." *Papers from the Eranos Yearbooks*, vol. 6. ed. Joseph Campbell. New York: Bollingen Foundation, 1968, pp. 375-415.

Nietzsche, Friedrich. *Saemtliche Werke: Kritische Studienausgabe in 15 Baenden.* Berlin: Deutscher Taschenbuch Verlag de Gruyter, 1967.

——. *Birth of Tragedy.* tr. Walter Kaufmann. New York: Vintage Books, 1967.

——. *Will to Power.* trs. Walter Kaufmann and R. J. Hollingdale. New York: Vintage Books, 1968.

——. *Beyond Good and Evil.* tr. Walter Kaufmann. New York: Random House, 1966.

——. *The Genealogy of Morals.* tr. Francis Golffing. New York: Doubleday, 1956.

Norris, Christopher. *Deconstruction: Theory and Practice.* London: Routledge, 1982.

Northrop, F. S. C. *The Meeting of East and West.* New York: Macmillan, 1960.

Nuttall, Jeff. *Bomb Culture.* New York: Delacorte Press, 1968.

Nygren, Anders. *Agape and Eros.* Philadelphia: Westminster Press, 1953.

Orman, John. *The Politics of Rock Music.* Chicago: Nelson-Hall, 1984.

Otto, Walter. *Dionysus: Myth and Cult.* tr. Robert Palmer, Bloomington: Indiana University Press, 1965.

Pattison, Robert. *The Triumph of Vulgarity.* Oxford: Oxford University Press, 1987.

Pickard-Cambridge, A. W. *Dithyramb: Tragedy and Comedy.* Oxford: Clarendon Press, 1962.

Pirsig, Robert. *Zen and the Art of Motorcycle Maintenance.* New York: Bantam Books, 1974.

Plato: The Collected Works. eds. Edith Hamilton and Huntington Cairnes. Princeton: Princeton University Press, 1961.

Reich, Charles. *The Greening of America.* New York: Random House, 1970.

Roszak, Theodore. *The Making of a Counter-Culture.* New York: Doubleday, 1969.

——. *Person/Planet: The Creative Disintegration of Industrial Society.* New York: Anchor Press, 1978.

——. *Where the Wasteland Ends: Politics and Transcendence in Postindustrial Society.* Garden City, NY: Doubleday, 1972.

——. *Unfinished Animal: The Aquarian Frontier and the Evolution of Consciousness.* New York: Harper and Row, 1975.

——. *The Voice of the Earth.* New York: Simon and Schuster, 1992.

——. "Beyond the Reality Principle." *Sierra* (March/April 1993), pp. 59-62 and 80.

—— and Betty Roszak. *Masculine/Feminine: Readings in Sexual Mythology and the Liberation of Women.* New York: Harper and Row, 1969.

Scheler, Max. *The Nature of Sympathy.* New Haven: Yale University Press, 1954.

Schilpp, P. A., ed. *Albert Einstein: Philosopher-Scientist.* New York: Tudor, 1954.

Segal, Robert. *Joseph Campbell: An Introduction.* New York: Penguin Books, 1990.

Sessions, Robert. "Deep Ecology versus Ecofeminism: Healthy Differences or Incompatible Philosophies?," *Hypatia* vol. 6, no. 1 (Spring 1991), pp. 90-107.

Sheppard, R. Z. "The Enormous Vroom," *Time* (April 15, 1974), pp. 99-105.

Tarnas, Richard. *The Passion of the Western Mind.* New York: Ballantine Books, 1993.

Thurin, Erik. *Emerson as Priest of Pan.* Lawrence: The Regents Press of Kansas, 1981.

Todd, Richard. "Praise God, From Whom All Ball Bearings Flow." *Atlantic Review* (May 1974), pp. 92-94.

Waggoner, Hyatt, ed. *Hawthorne: Selected Tales and Sketches.* New York: Rinehart, 1970.

Ward, Ed, Geoffrey Stokes, and Ken Tucker. *Rock of Ages: The Rolling Stone History of Rock and Roll.* New York: Summit Books, 1986.

Watts, Alan. *Tao: The Watercourse Way.* New York: Pantheon Books, 1975.

——. *Nature, Man, and Woman.* New York: Vintage Books, 1970.

——. *Beyond Theology: The Art of Godmanship.* New York: Vintage Books, 1973.

——. *This Is It, and Other Essays on Zen and Spiritual Experience.* New York: Collier Books, 1967.

——. *The Two Hands of God: The Myths of Polarity.* New York: G. Braziller, 1968.

——. *In My Own Way: An Autobiography.* New York: Pantheon Books, 1972.

——. *The Joyous Cosmology: Adventures in the Chemistry of Consciousness.* New York: Pantheon Books, 1962.

——. *Psychotherapy East and West.* New York: Ballantine Books, 1970.

Wilber, Ken. *Eye to Eye: The Quest for the New Paradigm.* New York: Anchor Books, 1983.

——. *The Spectrum of Consciousness.* Wheaton, Il.: Theosophical Publishing House, 1977.

Wenner, Jann. *Lennon Remembers: The Rolling Stone Interviews.* San Francisco: Straight Arrow Books, 1971.

Wilamowitz-Moellendorf, Ulrich. *Greek Historical Writing and Apollo.* tr. Gilbert Murray. Oxford: Oxford University Press, 1903.

Yoder, R. A. *Emerson and the Orphic Poet in America.* Berkeley: University of California Press, 1978.

Discography

The Beatles. "Tomorrow Never Knows." *Revolver.* Capitol Records, 1966.

——. "It's All Too Much." *Yellow Submarine.* Apple Records, 1969.

——. *Sergeant Pepper's Lonely Hearts Club Band.* Capitol Records, 1967.

——. *Magical Mystery Tour.* Capitol Records, 1967.

——. "Here Comes the Sun." *Abbey Road.* Apple Records, 1969.

——. "The Sun King." *Abbey Road.* Apple Records, 1969.

——. "Across the Universe." *Let It Be.* Apple Records, 1970.

The Byrds. "Eight Miles High." *Fifth Dimension.* Columbia Records, 1966.

Donovan. "Sunshine Superman." *Donovan's Greatest Hits.* Epic Records, 1968.

The Doors "The End." *The Doors.* Elektra Records, 1967.

——. "Waiting for the Sun." *Morrison Hotel.* Elektra Records, 1970.

Dylan, Bob. "All Along the Watchtower." *John Wesley Harding*. Columbia Records, 1968.

——. "Blowin' in the Wind." *Bob Dylan's Greatest Hits*. Columbia Records, 1967.

——. "The Times They Are A-Changin'." *Bob Dylan's Greatest Hits*. Columbia Records, 1967.

——. "Mr. Tambourine Man." *Bob Dylan's Greatest Hits*. Columbia Records, 1967.

Fifth Dimension. "Aquarius/Let the Sunshine In." *The Age of Aquarius*. Bell Records, 1969.

Gabriel, Peter. "Solsbury Hill." *Peter Gabriel*. Charisma Records, 1977.

The Grateful Dead. "Brokedown Palace." *American Beauty*. Warner Brothers, 1970.

——. "Ripple." *American Beauty*. Warner Brothers Records, 1970.

——. "Uncle John's Band." *Workingman's Dead*. Warner Brothers Records, 1970.

——. "Eyes of the World." *Wake of the Flood*. Grateful Dead Records, 1973.

——. "Here Comes Sunshine." *Wake of the Flood*. Grateful Dead Records, 1973.

The Guess Who. "No Sugar Tonight/New Mother Nature." *American Woman*. RCA Records, 1970.

Hendrix, Jimi. "Purple Haze." *Are You Experienced?* Reprise Records, 1968.

Jefferson Airplane. "White Rabbit." *Surrealistic Pillow*. RCA Records, 1967.

Moody Blues. *In Search of the Lost Chord.* London Records, 1968.

——. "Dawning Is the Day." *A Question of Balance.* London Records, 1970.

Morrison, Van. "Into the Mystic." *Moondance.* Warner Brothers, 1970.

Rolling Stones. "(I Can't Get No) Satisfaction." *Out of Our Heads.* London Records, 1965.

——. "Paint It Black." *Aftermath.* London Records, 1966.

——. "Sympathy for the Devil." *Beggar's Banquet.* London Records, 1968.

——. "Street Fighting Man." *Beggar's Banquet.* London Records, 1968.

——. *Their Satanic Majesties Request.* London Records, 1967.

Spirit. "Nature's Way." *The Best of Spirit.* Epic Records, 1973.

Steely Dan. "Home at Last." *Aja.* ABC Records, 1977.

Young, Neil. "Love in Mind." *Love in Mind.* Broken Arrow Music, 1971.